NEVER
THE
TWAIN
SHALL
MEET

NEVER
THE
TWAIN
SHALL
MEET

Bell, Gallaudet, and the Communications Debate

RICHARD WINEFIELD

Gallaudet University Press
Washington, D.C.

Photo credits: Photographs of Alexander Graham Bell, members of the Bell family, and the Visible Speech chart and glove, courtesy of the Library of Congress. Photographs of Edward Miner Gallaudet, members of the Gallaudet family, the American School for the Deaf, and the *Silent Echo*, courtesy of the Gallaudet University Archives.

Gallaudet University Press, Washington, DC 20002
© 1987 by Gallaudet University. All rights reserved
Published 1987
Printed in the United States of America

Library of Congress Cataloging-in-Publication Data

Winefield, Richard, 1949–
    Never the twain shall meet.

    Bibliography: p.
    Includes index.
    1. Deaf—United States—Means of communication.
2. Children, Deaf—Education—United States.   3. Bell,
Alexander Graham, 1847–1922.   4. Gallaudet, Edward
Miner, 1837–1917.   I. Title.
HV2471.W56   1987   362.4′283   87-11885
ISBN 0-913580-99-6

Gallaudet University is an equal opportunity employer/educational institution. Programs and services offered by Gallaudet University receive substantial financial support from the U.S. Department of Education.

Oh, East is East, and West is West, and never
the twain shall meet,
Till Earth and Sky stand presently at God's
great Judgment Seat;
But there is neither East nor West, border,
nor breed, nor birth,
When two strong men stand face to face,
though they come from the ends of the earth!

Rudyard Kipling
The Ballad of East and West (1889)

Contents

Acknowledgments

DOING HISTORICAL RESEARCH provides many pleasures, not least of which is tracking down some elusive citation in a dark, dust-covered corner of a forgotten archive. An even greater satisfaction comes from the use of that information in the forming of an original historical analysis or interpretation. This is solitary work, and it can be a lonely experience. Thus, in thanking those who have helped me I include not only those who helped create the final product, but those who kept me sane along the way.

My research necessitated travel to numerous libraries and archives, and everywhere I went I was greeted by enthusiastic and supportive people. My thanks to the Clarke School for the Deaf in Northampton, Massachusetts; the Manuscript Division of the Library of Congress in Washington, D.C.; and the library staffs at Gallaudet University in Washington, D.C., and the Gutman Library at Harvard University. I especially acknowledge the assistance of Gallaudet University archivists David L. de Lorenzo and Corrine Hilton.

A number of scholars in the fields of history and social policy provided me with valuable insights and ideas. Robert Bruce and Maxine Tull Boatner gave me important primary source locations; Deborah Klein-Walker and Sheldon White kept me on track while constantly renewing my creative energy. Joseph Featherstone's involvement, both conceptual and editorial, resulted in a more readable and substantial work.

Numerous parents and teachers shared their time and emotions with me as interview subjects. These interviews were confidential, and so the subjects must remain anonymous. Our discussions were important in proving to me that the attitudes and expectations of nineteenth-century educators (such as Bell and Gallaudet) were alive and well in the twentieth century.

Jeanne Menary and Margery Somers reviewed and edited preliminary drafts of this book, and I thank them for their honesty and forthrightness. Ivey Pittle and Jim Stentzel, my editors at Gallaudet University Press, got more out of me than I thought I had. Sarah Levine edited my writing, buoyed my spirits, and through her example showed me how a first-rate thesis should be written. Her curried chicken is similarly outstanding.

Finally, I save my greatest thanks for my wife and parents. Their encouragement and support were important, but more than that, their love served as a constant reminder that no book, and perhaps no thing, is more important than family. Emily Louise Winefield died prior to the publication of this book, and I dedicate it to her memory.

Preface

THE SUBJECT OF THIS BOOK is deaf children and the way in which they communicate and are educated. More specifically, I am interested in the reasons for the debate over the use of sign language with these children.

This book is not intended to be supportive of either signing or oralism. My focus is on a different set of questions: How did the debate begin? and Why, after so many years, does it continue? To answer these questions, I have concentrated on the nineteenth century, especially the two men who set the course that has since been followed by proponents of both communication methods. By studying Alexander Graham Bell and Edward Miner Gallaudet and the feelings and attitudes that influenced their actions, I hope to add a new perspective to the sign language discussion. And if Bell's and Gallaudet's actions continue to influence today's educational practices, might not the reasons behind their actions still have relevance as well?

From 1972 through 1977 my life was occupied with teaching deaf children. As a teacher I met and worked with many wonderful students, teachers, and administrators—both hearing and deaf. At the same time, I was dismayed by the easy acceptance of outmoded and destructive teaching methods, distressed at the ineptness of uncaring policymakers, and disturbed by the lack of foresight and vision at all levels of the educational hierarchy. This situation can be illustrated by looking at the communication methods used with two of my former students.

Jimmy was *Mr. Popularity* in the school; he was a good athlete; a good thinker; and a friendly, outgoing fellow. He experienced few problems during his elementary and secondary school years. His biggest problem, if it can be called that, was his minimal hearing loss. Jimmy could hear almost, but not quite, as well as someone with normal hearing. He was a perfect candidate for an oral program (one in which speech and speechreading are used to teach language). Instead, Jimmy languished in a residential school where sign language was the principal means of communication. His reading, writing, and math skills were good compared to those of his fellow students, but these same skills were low compared to those of public school children. Why hadn't this boy been placed in a more appropriate setting, closer to the mainstream of

normally hearing children where expectations were higher and opportunities for growth more numerous? Had his best interests been considered by those around him?

Jimmy's story may have a happy ending because his ability to make
friends, along with his good oral skills (no thanks to his old school), will
probably enable him to do well. Susan's story may also end happily,
though her road has been as rough as any imaginable.

The birth of a deaf daughter to Susan's parents was the beginning
of the end for their marriage. The father blamed the mother for the
birth of what they both considered to be a deformed child. The mother
accepted the blame and the guilt. These parents chose an oral program
for Susan so that she would look, act, and speak like a normal child.
They rejected sign language as well as the idea that anything about Susan
was different or bad. Susan's parents simply denied the handicap of
deafness.

Years came and went and Susan made little progress. Academically
she was below average and, despite hundreds of hours of training, her
speech and speechreading skills were minimal. She had few friends and
could barely communicate with her own family. Her breaking point
came one day, in the middle of a lesson she couldn't understand. She
started to cry, and no one—not her teacher, her classmates, nor her
counselor—could help her to stop, and it was in that state that she was
taken home.

When Susan's mother decided to put Susan into a classroom where
sign language was used, Susan's father threatened to leave home. Susan
was transferred, and her father left. The change in Susan was astonishing;
she learned sign language in record time. Within a week she was communicating with children her own age for the first time in her life.
Within a month she was sharing secrets with the other girls, and soon
after had her first boyfriend. As Susan's teacher I was amazed at what
I saw and could easily forgive her preference for gossip over geography.
She had a lot of catching up to do!

Both of these stories, while simplified versions of complex situations,
indicate an inability or unwillingness to deal with deaf children in terms
of their own needs and capabilities. In 1880 this was understandable, as
education for deaf children was in its infancy. But in the 1970s? While I saw
many talented and dedicated people in my profession, I also saw archaic
and ill-conceived policies and practices, and teachers and administrators

unable or unwilling to improve them. For all I knew my own efforts were adding to the problem.

I now have the advantage of distance and time in which to study the situation. My hope is that this book will help me understand the field of deaf education and exorcise my own feelings of guilt and inadequacy for having left it. If, in the process, I reveal new insights that will help educators and parents, I will have succeeded beyond my more modest aspirations.

My greatest strength as a writer on this subject could be, in another way, a weakness. As a trained and experienced teacher of deaf children, I have had direct contact with students, parents, teachers, and administrators. However, my experience has been almost entirely in an environment that values sign language. I have tried to write a fair account; however, I will leave it to readers to render a verdict on my success. My conscience has already passed judgment, and only its favorable decision allowed for this book's publication.

One other strength and weakness requires note. I contend that the heart of the communication debate rests with attitudes and expectations—characteristics that influenced and continue to influence actions and thoughts. The strength is that this is a subject in need of investigation. The weakness is that it propels me near to the border of my own expertise, as I am not a psychologist. While this does not disqualify me from writing psychohistory, it does require that I emphasize the history and tread lightly on the psychology. I am comforted by Erik Erikson's advice in his classic *Young Man Luther* (New York: W. W. Norton, 1962):

> We may have to risk that bit of impurity which is inherent in the hyphen of the psycho-historical as well as of all other hyphenated approaches. They are the compost heap of today's interdisciplinary efforts, which may help to fertilize new fields, and to produce future flowers of new methodological clarity. (p. 16)

Thus buoyed by Erikson, mindful of my limits and biases, and wary of the compost heap—I proceed.

Prologue

SUMMERS IN FLINT WERE ALWAYS HOT, and the summer of 1895 was no exception. Perhaps the temperature had something to do with the heat being generated in the convention hall, for what had started as simply a gathering of teachers of deaf children had turned into high drama.

There was always the chance of a major confrontation when these two men got together, but what had transpired during the last week had surprised everyone. First the leader of oral education, Alexander Graham Bell, made the standard speech emphasizing cooperation and unity. His archrival, sign language proponent Edward Miner Gallaudet, was expected to do the same. Instead, he blasted Bell and everything he stood for, stunning the convention audience by questioning Bell's honesty and integrity and blaming him for the current schism within the field of education of deaf children. Certainly the two disagreed about how best to communicate with deaf children, but their disagreement had never taken such a nasty turn, at least not publicly.

Bell rebutted the charges made against him. He succeeded or failed depending on one's point of view. His allies, supporters of oralism, characterized his speech as "inspired" and "delightful." Sign language proponents, however, called it "lame" and "impotent." Thus, the stage was set for another confrontation when the delegates took their seats for the convention's last session.

The convention hall was steaming when Dr. Mathieson (from the Ontario School for the Deaf) rose and walked to the podium. "Let there be peace," he intoned, and motioned Bell and Gallaudet to the front. At first, neither man moved. Then, at the urging of those around them, the two men began walking toward each other. They had feuded for years, but now their relationship had hit rock bottom. How could they possibly make peace?

The delegates became silent as the two men approached one another, their footsteps echoing through the hall. People in the back rows stood for a better view. When Bell and Gallaudet were within arm's reach, each man, without smiling, extended his right hand. The tips of their fingers barely touched in the most frigid of handshakes. Then, without speaking, each man turned and walked away. A plea had been made for peace, but a different message had been given. Henceforth, signers and oralists would take different paths. The last chance to unify the field had been lost, resulting in many more years of antagonism and frustration for teachers, parents, and deaf children.

NEVER
THE
TWAIN
SHALL
MEET

O N E

American Asylum for the Deaf and Dumb,
Hartford, Connecticut; ca. 1850

The Communications Debate

T
HE problems involved in raising and educating deaf children
have been discussed since the time of Aristotle, but only in the
last two hundred years have real efforts been made to develop
formal educational programs for them. Throughout these two centuries,
one question has constantly plagued those in the field of education of
the deaf—Should sign language be used to communicate with and instruct deaf children? This question has been argued with intense conviction by policymakers, teachers, linguists, and parents, yet it remains
unanswered to this day. Deaf children, meanwhile, have been stuck in
the middle of the debate, buffeted to and fro by each new wave of
opinion and controversy. Why, after two centuries, does the disagreement
remain unresolved?

This book attempts to answer that question and, in the process, raises
some compelling possibilities. The focus will be on the nineteenth century, when the sign language debate was at its highest pitch and the

battlelines were clearly drawn. During this time, two men served as leaders of the opposing sides. Alexander Graham Bell (1847–1922), the inventor of the telephone, led the fight against the use of sign language; he supported the use of speech and speechreading. His rival, Edward Miner Gallaudet (1837–1917), was the leading advocate for the use of sign language. Each man had a different theory about how deaf children should be taught. Until now, these theories have been accepted as the reason for Bell and Gallaudet's disagreement over sign language. However, careful study of each man's family background, expectations for the deaf, and attitude toward deviance tells a different story. These factors were crucial in determining Bell's and Gallaudet's ideas and actions.

The first few chapters examine how Bell and Gallaudet opposed each other in their roles as champions of the different methods of teaching deaf children. This requires a close look at their political styles, their frequent and dramatic confrontations, and their stormy personal relationship. The later chapters explore some of the reasons why the men clung so fervently to their particular philosophies. Their deep commitments can only be explained by examining their very powerful beliefs.

Both Bell and Gallaudet kept journals and diaries, and Bell preserved a large collection of private correspondence. These primary sources serve as the foundation for this book. What emerges is a portrait of two men who both served education of the deaf as great benefactors and as destructive forces. Their differing philosophies, specifically their expectations for the education and placement of deaf persons in the hearing world, are important factors in the nineteenth-century communications debate. The real cause of Bell and Gallaudet's feud, however, may be their attitudes toward deviance and society. These same attitudes may also be the cause of the sign language debate as it exists today.

Oral vs. Combined Education

The controversy that divided Bell and Gallaudet still exists today among educators of the deaf. This philosophical debate is, and always has been, over the best way to communicate with and teach deaf students. The two philosophical camps are composed of advocates of the oral method and the combined method. The major difference between the two methods centers around the use of sign language.

The oral philosophy was founded on the premise that almost all people process language auditorally. Oralists have always believed that deaf people must be prepared to live as much like hearing people as possible. Therefore, children in oral programs were, and still are, taught to communicate through speech and speechreading (carefully monitoring the lips and facial movements of people speaking to them). Children in oral programs are also taught to make use of their residual hearing through hearing aids. The formal use of sign language is not allowed in oral programs.

The manual philosophy was based on the belief that many deaf children could not learn to speak or speechread well enough to have it be their primary means of communication. Early manualists advocated only the use of sign language for communication and instruction. Later, however, largely through the efforts of Edward Miner Gallaudet, speech became an integral part of communication instruction. This method has come to be known as the combined method. Children in combined programs are taught to sign, speak, speechread, and make use of their residual hearing.

American Sign Language (ASL), the language used by the majority of deaf, signing adults in the United States, has a different grammatical structure than English. Many educators have found it difficult to use ASL in the classroom because it is not possible to sign in ASL and speak English at the same time. In addition, it is difficult to teach students English when using a language with a different grammatical base. For these, and other reasons, different sign language systems have developed over the years in an effort to replicate English grammar. Proponents of the combined method believe that deaf students can fully develop their intellectual potential only through the use of sign language in the classroom and elsewhere. Proponents of the oral method claim that the use of sign language limits deaf people's ability to make contact with the larger hearing world.

It is difficult to describe the intensity of the nineteenth-century debate between combinists and oralists because it was so heated and, at times, irrational. More than a simple disagreement among educators, the argument impeded the education of children, destroyed friendships, and literally caused the breakup of entire families. Bell described the state of affairs as it existed at the turn of the century as follows:

It is hardly an exaggeration to say that oral teachers and sign teachers found it difficult to sit down in the same room without quarreling; and there was intolerance upon both sides. To say "oral method" to a sign teacher was like waving a red flag in the face of a bull! and to say "sign language" to an oralist aroused the deepest resentment.

On the one hand the sign teachers, who were largely men, looked down upon the oralists as visionary enthusiasts pursuing impracticable schemes. They honestly believed that the idea of teaching congenital Deaf-mutes to speak and read the lips was absurd, and they therefore considered the oralists as little better than charlatans pretending to accomplish the impossible. Equally impossible and absurd appeared the idea that Deaf-mutes could be educated without the use of the sign language and they even questioned the veracity of those who asserted the contrary.

On the other hand the oral teachers, who were largely women, were not a bit behind the others in the intensity of their feelings. The idea of teaching Deaf-mutes to speak appealed to them as a holy cause. They threw themselves into the work with all the zeal of religious fanatics. They were glad to become martyrs in such a cause; and I have no doubt that some of them would even have been willing to lay down their lives if need be, in order that the Deaf and Dumb should be taught to speak. They considered it actually a crime to deprive a deaf child of the power of articulate speech by neglecting to instruct him in the use of his vocal organs—A crime aggravated by teaching him a special language, peculiar to Deaf-mutes, that prevented him from mingling with his fellows of the hearing world and made of deaf children a race apart.[1]

A Short History
of the Education of Deaf Children

In 1895 the oralists were led by Alexander Graham Bell, the combinists by Edward Miner Gallaudet. However, the debate over communication methods began well before their time. The problems of deaf people had been studied by Socrates, Aristotle, and St. Augustine; it was not until the sixteenth century, though, that any real efforts were made to teach the deaf.

  Pablo Ponce de Leon, a Spanish monk, is generally credited as being the first teacher of deaf children. During the time he lived in a Benedictine monastery in San Salvador, he met a man who had been denied the monastic life due to his deafness. Ponce de Leon was able to teach this man to read and speak well enough to be accepted as a postulant. Some years later, Ponce de Leon established a school north of Madrid where he tutored deaf children who were "sons of great lords and of notable people."[2]

Little is known of Ponce de Leon's methods or even whether he used sign language. Consequently, historians have disagreed over the methods he used; for example, Hodgson claimed that Ponce de Leon did use signs,[3] while Bender wrote that he used oral methods.[4] From these two examples, it appears that the methods argument began not with Ponce de Leon, but with those who wrote of his work.

The first educator to state a clear preference for a communication method was Juan Pablo Bonet, also a Spaniard. In 1620 he wrote the first book on educating deaf students; he advocated the use of manual communication along with early instruction in speech and academic subjects.[5] Bonet's signs took the form of one-handed fingerspelling, much like that used in the United States today. Once a student had learned the sign for a letter, the actual sound would be studied. Speech and signing were not separated. Bonet and his contemporary, Manuel Ramirez de Carrion, argued over who had actually developed this method of instruction, but all agreed that it was successful. This success was hard to duplicate, however, since it required long-term, individualized, and costly instruction.[6]

From the early 1600s to 1755 the way deaf students and their teachers communicated was not an issue; most educators advocated speech instruction along with some form of manual communication. Signs and gestures were not always a formal part of the curriculum, but neither were they prohibited. Instruction in lipreading (or speechreading, as it is now called) was uncommon until Johann Amman, a doctor who worked with deaf children in Holland, reported positive results in 1700.

The situation changed, and polarization began, with the work of Abbé Charles Michel de l'Epée. De l'Epée (1712–1789) founded the world's first public school for deaf children in Paris in 1755. He was greatly influenced by the sign language used by deaf people in France at that time. De l'Epée, an abbé in the Catholic church, thought that by teaching deaf children to communicate he could enable them to take their vows and, thereby, save their souls. Believing that sign language was the natural way deaf people communicated their ideas, he incor-

porated it into his school's curriculum. Over time, de l'Epée formalized
the sign language to make it more compatible with standard French.
While he did not specifically condemn the teaching of speech and speechreading, he did not emphasize it. Under him and his successor, Abbé
Roch Ambroise Sicard (1742–1822), the use of sign language gradually
supplanted almost all use of speech. The Paris school became a manual
environment.

This deemphasis of oral skills in France was attacked by the educators in Germany. Samuel Heinicke, considered the father of the German oral method, believed that methodical signs were detrimental to
the effective instruction of deaf students.[7] In 1778, he opened a school
for deaf children with the stated goal of integrating them into German
society. His school used oral methods exclusively. John Graser (1766–
1841), a vocal opponent of the French method, emphasized the importance of integrating deaf students with hearing students. For this reason,
the oral method was the only method he allowed his students to use.
Through his efforts, many deaf students were placed in regular classrooms. Frederick Hill (1805–1874), probably the most influential of the
German educators of the deaf, was one of the first teachers to actually
prohibit students from using sign language. He believed strongly that
signing hindered the natural acquisition of language. Through Hill and
the teachers he trained, the oral method became the method of choice
in Germany and in much of Europe.

The first school for deaf students in the United States was founded
in Hartford, Connecticut, in 1817. This school, the American Asylum
for the Education of the Deaf and Dumb, was for the most part a manual
school. Its founder, Thomas Hopkins Gallaudet (1787–1851) had intended to employ a combined communication approach, but an interesting set of circumstances prevented this outcome. In 1815, a small
group of Hartford businessmen raised funds to send someone to Europe
to study the different methods of teaching deaf students. This person
was to return to the United States and establish a school based on the
best of the European techniques. Gallaudet, a young seminarian with
an interest in deafness, consented to make the trip. His first stop was
the Braidwood school in Great Britain. However, his efforts to study
the oral methods in use there were rebuffed. The Braidwoods preferred
neither to divulge the secrets of their trade nor to share the spotlight
with Sicard and the French school, which was to be Gallaudet's next

stop. Perhaps most importantly, the Braidwoods may have been protecting the interests of John Braidwood, who was then in the United States to establish his own school.

After leaving the Braidwood school, Gallaudet traveled to Paris and the Royal School for Deaf-Mutes, the school founded by Abbé de l'Epée. Its director, Abbé Sicard, greeted Gallaudet warmly and encouraged him to stay for more than the three months he had planned on. During this time Gallaudet observed in classrooms, learned sign language, and had private lessons on the instruction of deaf children from Sicard's assistant, Jean Massieu. When Gallaudet returned to the United States he was accompanied by Laurent Clerc, a teacher in the Paris school. Clerc became the first deaf person to teach deaf students in the United States. He stayed at the American Asylum as an instructor for many years, and he was a forceful and articulate opponent of oral education.

Though Gallaudet had tried to learn both oral and manual methods on his trip, he returned with knowledge in only one area. Thus, this country's first school for deaf children, while not entirely foregoing instruction in speech, would most accurately be described as a manual school. There is some dispute over whether Gallaudet had ever intended to learn both methods. Robert Bruce, in a biography of Bell, claims that Thomas Gallaudet chose the French model partly due to Braidwood's secrecy and "partly because the 'oral method' made heavier demands on the pupil's intelligence, alertness and perseverance."[8] This statement implies that oralism is best, but only for students smart enough to use it. The truth is, no research then or since has linked success in oral programs to intelligence, nor has careful study revealed that this was the reason behind Gallaudet's choice of methods. One thing does seem certain—Thomas Gallaudet's belief in the effectiveness of sign language had a major impact on his son Edward.

Gallaudet was not the only American to travel abroad in search of methods for teaching deaf children. In 1843 Horace Mann and Samuel Gridley Howe, two well-known American educators, went to Germany for that same purpose. They returned from this trip convinced of the need to establish an oral school in the United States. Their report ignited a firestorm over the question of methods.

Representatives from both the American Asylum and the New York School for the Deaf traveled to Germany to observe the oral method in the 1840s. In contrast to Mann and Howe, their reports were critical.

Lewis Weld, from the American Asylum, reported that even in the "purely oral" schools of Germany natural signs were used to instruct children. Mann and Howe had reported seeing classes where nothing but speech was used, but Weld felt sure they had been duped. Mann and Howe, he wrote,

> had fully believed in the truth of their assertions, because on their visiting a few of these schools as foreign travellers, they have probably been entertained, not by witnessing much of the process of instruction, but by hearing the drilled exercises of the pupils in articulation; which, with other matters intended expressly for visitors, are too often prepared and kept ready for use on all such occasions.[9]

In addition, Weld claimed that the German schools were highly selective in their admissions standards and were quick to "remove unworthy members and those whose deficiencies forbid their making any decidedly valuable attainments, especially if they are supported by charity."[10] Weld's accusation that oral schools guaranteed their own success by accepting only those students likely to do well—though students' lack of oral skills might be overlooked with the proper tuition payment—is still voiced by some critics of oral education.

Despite Weld's counterattack, after 1843 the demand for oral schools grew. The first oral schools, however, were not established until the 1860s. The New York Institution for the Improved Instruction of Deaf-Mutes (now the Lexington School for the Deaf) and the Clarke Institution for Deaf-Mutes (in Northampton, Massachusetts) were the first oral schools for deaf children in the United States. The Clarke School is particularly important for this study because it is where Alexander Graham Bell gained entrée into the world of deafness.

This historical summary has highlighted only a few of the many individuals who influenced the spread and acceptance of different communication methods. The history has its dark side, too; new methods of instruction or communication were often kept secret for fear that others would steal them. However, this dark side is outweighed by evidence of great dedication and even heroism. The important fact to note here is that the debate between signers and oralists is an old one, and it was already old when Bell and Gallaudet assumed leadership of the two ideological armies.

Current Perspectives

Some scholars claim that the communications debate is rooted in politics. Donald Moores equates the rise of different teaching methods with the changing international political scene. For example, Spain was a powerful force in world affairs during the 1500s, perhaps explaining that country's influence in the education of deaf people. In the seventeenth century Great Britain emerged as an important influence, both in world politics and in education of the deaf. The ascendance of the oral method is described as being coincidental with "rising German political influence and the smashing German military victory in the Franco-Prussian War."[11] According to this theory, the future ascendancy of oralism or sign language will be determined by the outcome of diplomatic battles between the United States and the Soviet Union.

This theory does make sense. Until recently, the education of deaf children was in its infancy. People making major contributions to the field were notable for their *firsts*—first teacher, first school, first stated philosophy. It is not surprising that these individuals were from countries that were also in the forefront of world events since such countries had the resources, as well as the values, necessary to foster innovative thinkers.

The picture today, however, is quite different. Many countries, not just the United States and the Soviet Union, have highly trained and committed educators and researchers with an interest in deafness. Countries are now less likely to look to the United States for examples, either in the educational or the political spheres of action. The state of U.S.–Soviet affairs will clearly have an impact on the rest of the world, but it is unlikely that countries such as France, Great Britain, or West Germany will choose a communication method on the basis of political considerations. Countries in the Soviet sphere of influence, particularly those nations relying on the Soviets for technical expertise and resources, may indeed import an oral philosophy because the majority of Soviet schools for deaf children are oral.

When the focus changes from international to state and local levels, the link between politics and communication philosophies becomes more clear-cut. As governments reduce spending for education, as they have in the 1980s, they must sometimes make a communications choice. A state that funds two large schools, one oral and the other combined, may close one to save money. When the Connecticut legislature was faced with this choice, it closed the oral school. Legislators there considered many things when making their choice, including educational, fiscal, geographic, and personal factors. The blending of these factors into a single decision provided Connecticut's oralists with a painful lesson in the political process.

Lawmakers in Massachusetts have had a tremendous influence on the choice of communication methods in that state. Indeed, for many years parents and teachers were actually denied a choice between communication methods. Chapter 69, Section 28 of the Massachusetts General Laws stipulated that all students in special classes be provided lipreading instruction. At the time of this law's passage in 1923, only oral programs provided such instruction; so, the law was actually a mandate for oralism. Parents who insisted on another method were forced to move to another state or send their children to a residential school in another state. Here was political influence at its most obvious, and perhaps at its worst. One need not be a proponent of any one system to understand that no system is best for all children. Yet, lobbyists for oral education and their allies in the statehouse in Boston imposed one system on all deaf children in the state. Only in the last ten years has legislation on the national and state levels provided for instruction with sign language for those families choosing it.

While the history of the communications debate may have been affected by politics, there were clearly other factors of equal or greater importance. A knowledge of this history does show that neither Bell nor Gallaudet actually caused the wide rift that obviously existed between oralists and combinists. Their positions as leaders did give them the opportunity to narrow it, and each man often expressed a desire to do exactly that. Their inability to succeed at making peace doomed the field to years of unfriendly competition and raised the question that educators continue to ask today: Will it ever be possible for oralists and combinists to work together?

Alexander Graham Bell, 1864

The Education of an Oralist

B Y any standard, Alexander Graham (A. G.) Bell was a remarkable man. He possessed unquenchable curiosity, boundless energy, great dignity, superior intelligence and creativity, and a remarkable sense of confidence in his ability to take on problems and solve them. Of his many interests, none received more of his attention than the education of deaf children. His success in this field, added to the prestige he gained in the scientific world, made him the perfect standard-bearer for the oral movement. Whatever one's views of oralism, it is certain that Bell, more than anyone else, popularized and legitimized the oral philosophy in the United States. As a result of his early successes with Visible Speech, his tireless efforts to promote oral education within the field of deafness and in the political arena, and his financial and moral support, Bell surely qualifies as the nineteenth century's most important leader in oral education for deaf children.

Early Influences

Bell was born in Edinburgh, Scotland, in 1847. Despite his great fame and influence in the world, much of what is commonly known about him is more fiction than fact. For instance, it is generally accepted that the first utterance on the telephone was a distress call. Bell, the story goes, spilled acid on himself and called through the phone to his assistant, "Mr. Watson, come here, I want you." No acid was actually spilled, but the myth lives on—as if so dramatic an event requires embellishment. Bell's work as an educator of deaf children has also been fictionalized on occasion. As with the telephone, however, the actual facts paint him as an important figure without need of elaboration.

Bell's first exposure to deafness came from his hearing-impaired mother. Eliza Bell had lost much of her hearing during childhood, but she had good speech and excellent language skills. A factor contributing to her skill in these areas is the strong likelihood that her deafness was severe but not profound. Though accurate hearing testing had not yet begun (Bell didn't invent the necessary apparatus until 1879), records show that Eliza Bell used an ear trumpet, taught her sons to play the piano, and actually played the piano herself. She even took responsibility for educating her children at home—Alec (as his family called him) was not enrolled in school until he was ten years old. Eliza Bell's only handicap, as far as her deafness was concerned, was a difficulty in conducting conversations; she was a poor speechreader.

Many individuals cite their parents' or siblings' deafness as their impetus to working with deaf students. This was not the case with A. G. Bell. He was not interested in this kind of work until other circumstances arose. It is undeniable that his mother colored his view of oralism and sign language by providing an example of a happy, successful deaf woman who did not rely on manual communication. In spite of this influence, his father, Melville Bell, was his real link to the education of deaf students. Melville Bell, like his father before him, was an elocutionist (a teacher of oral delivery, including voice control and gestures), and he was intensely interested in the improvement of speech.

Melville Bell developed Visible Speech, a system that described oral sounds through written symbols, as a method for improving speech. In order to convince people of the benefits of Visible Speech, he gave public demonstrations of the method with his sons. At these demonstrations,

Visible Speech chart developed by Alexander Melville Bell in 1864.

the boys would leave the room, after which those present would recite passages or combinations of sounds, including those from various languages. Melville Bell would write down what was said using Visible Speech symbols, and the sons would then enter the room and proceed to read the symbols aloud, duplicating exactly what was said. One person who attended a demonstration later described it as follows:

> When Bell's sons had been sent away to another part of the house out of earshot, we gave Bell the most peculiar and difficult sounds we could think of, including words from the French and Gaelic, following these with inarticulate sounds, as of kissing, chuckling, etc. All these Bell wrote down in his Visible Speech alphabet, and his sons were then called in. I well remember our keen interest, and by and by, astonishment, as the lads ... reproduced the sounds faithfully; but like the ghost of its former self in its detachment from the stretching and body twisting with which it had originally been combined.[1]

While the Visible Speech system was not designed as a teaching technique for deaf students, its use in this regard was eventually discovered. The *London Illustrated Times*, describing a Visible Speech demonstration, commented that "We cannot pretend even to guess at the horizons opened up by such an alphabet in the training of the deaf, the dumb, and the blind."[2] Such newspaper comments, added to his own imagination, soon led Melville Bell to state that one of the uses of the system was in work with deaf students.

Susanna Hull, the director of a small school for deaf children in South Kensington, Great Britain, shared Bell's opinion. The Bell family was then living in Britain, and Hull came to them asking if the Visible Speech system could be used with her pupils. The responsibility fell to son Alexander, despite his total lack of experience or knowledge of how to teach deaf children. In May of 1868 he began working with two deaf pupils, and according to his journal he was almost immediately successful. After only one lesson the students were making sounds that were entirely new to them, and by the fifth lesson, they were supposedly uttering complete and intelligible sentences.

Teacher of Deaf Students

By 1870, Melville Bell had become a frequent lecturer on Visible Speech in Canada and the United States, and the Bell family had moved to

Brantford, Ontario. At one of his lectures, Sarah Fuller, director of the Boston School for Deaf-Mutes, became impressed with the possibilities Visible Speech held for deaf students. She asked Melville Bell if he would come to the school and teach Visible Speech to the pupils. He refused, but Alec accepted. A. G. Bell soon had a class of about thirty pupils and, as in South Kensington, success was almost immediate. By 1871 he was writing his parents that he was planning on the "establishment of a good profession" for himself at the school. He even began talking about founding a training school for teachers of deaf children.[3]

After summering with his family in Canada, A. G. Bell resumed teaching in Boston. It was then that he met and taught his first congenitally deaf pupil, Theresa Dudley. That his previous pupils had not been congenitally deaf raises the possibility that they were either hard of hearing or were deafened at a comparatively late age. This could account for his earlier quick and dramatic successes. Since speech was his only concern, and since residual hearing or prior speech skill greatly simplifies the task, Bell's early successes may have been overly dramatized. Indeed, Bell found his work with Dudley a new experience, one that required greater effort and time to achieve results. However, results did come, and when they did they were again dramatic, at least to Bell himself. He wrote to his parents, with his typical modesty, that his work with Dudley and others "constitutes an epoch in the History of Education of the Deaf and Dumb."[4] His enthusiasm and the support of other educators strengthened his desire to make the education of deaf children his life's work.

The communication controversy was very much a part of the education of deaf students in the late 1800s. Bell naturally gave it thought, and he came out in favor of oralism. This is hardly surprising, considering his emphasis on speech and articulation. However, he also came to believe that speech was an important skill. In this he disagreed with his own father. The elder Bell probably based his belief in the impracticality of speechreading on his experience with his own wife, who never could read lips. Despite A. G. Bell's tilt toward oralism, in 1872 he took training in sign language. Also in that year he accepted an invitation to visit and teach speech for two months at the American Asylum in Hartford.

This episode has been compared to Daniel entering the lion's den (Bell being an oralist and the American Asylum being a bastion of sign language). However, many educators who disagreed with Bell about the use of sign language, were, nonetheless, his admirers. The extent of the American Asylum administration's open-mindedness can be further demonstrated by their invitation to Bell to speak at commencement. Bell reciprocated this open-mindedness when he addressed the pupils in sign language.

Despite this apparent flexibility, Bell maintained a strong dislike for sign language, particularly when used without speech. Commenting on a pupil who, on his deathbed, refused to go home because no one there understood him, Bell stated, "Nothing can show better how the too great use of signs tends to isolate deaf-mutes and constitute a class apart from hearing people."[5] Throughout his life, Bell blamed sign language for the dissolution of families. Oral education, he claimed, would preserve families by ensuring ease of communication between deaf children and their parents. This belief eventually made Bell a leader in the movement to establish day schools for deaf students as alternatives to the more common residential schools.

In late 1872 Bell's inventive genius began asserting itself. At that time, he was working on the multiple telegraph, a device to allow the transmission of many messages through a single telegraph wire. This work was a tremendous drain on his time, and it limited his work with deaf children. However, he by no means abandoned teaching. By 1872 Bell had started working with George Sanders, a five-year-old deaf boy. When Bell went to stay with his own family in Ontario during the summer of 1873, Saunders went as well. And when Boston University made Bell a professor of vocal physiology and elocution, Sanders' grandmother gave Bell free room and board in her Salem home in return for continuing the instruction. The Sanders case is but a single example of Bell's dedication to his work with deaf students. No matter how far afield his interests spread, and regardless of the eventual demands made on his time during the development and patenting of the telephone, Bell continued to have an active interest in deafness.

Bell's relationship with George Sanders continued for many years, not only as teacher but also as friend and financial backer. However, one other teacher-student relationship that Bell made lasted longer and had far more consequences for both parties. Gardiner Greene Hubbard, a Boston lawyer and chair of the board of the Clarke School for the Deaf, knew of Bell's work with Visible Speech. Hubbard had a deaf daughter, and when Bell began private tutoring in 1873 to supplement his income, Hubbard enrolled her. Mabel Hubbard's first memories of Bell were not all positive.

> I both did not, and did like him. He was so interesting that I was forced to like to listen to him, but he himself I disliked. He dressed carelessly and in a horrible, shiny [hat]—expensive but fashionable—and which made his jet-black hair look shiny. Altogether I did not think him exactly a gentleman.[6]

Despite this initial impression, the relationship eventually culminated in a long and happy marriage. It also had a significant impact on Bell's approach to deaf education.

Gardiner Greene Hubbard's role in this account is not limited to his interest in educating deaf children and his relationship as Alexander Graham Bell's father-in-law. Hubbard and Bell shared another interest that overshadowed deafness—the development of the multiple telegraph. Before he had even met Bell, Hubbard had been active in efforts to make wider use of telegraphy. He was convinced that with lowered rates and improved technology telegrams could be sent like letters. Society would benefit and so would Hubbard, through the profits of his proposed United States Postal Telegraph Company. Unfortunately for Hubbard, Congress never authorized the company. When Thomas Edison invented a quadruplex telegraph that could carry four simultaneous messages over one wire and sold the rights to the Western Union Company, Hubbard's hopes were considerably dimmed. They were revived, however, by the coincidence of Bell's own interest in telegraphy. That Bell and Hubbard should have met is not surprising, given the link of deafness that existed. That both men were interested in telegraphy as well, the one as inventor and the other as promoter and financier, is indeed ironic. Hubbard eventually pinned all of his hopes for a profitable telegraph venture on A. G. Bell.

Hubbard became disturbed when Bell's interests and commitments expanded to include education, Visible Speech, telegraphy, telephony, and the wooing of his daughter. Hubbard wanted fast results in telegraphy, so, in 1874, he forced a choice on Bell. Bell could choose to work on telegraphy and have Mabel Hubbard's hand in marriage, with all living expenses taken care of, or he could teach deaf children and promote Visible Speech, but he would have to forgo the other options. Bell rejected this ultimatum. He refused to give up his work for the deaf, and he stood by his commitment to Visible Speech out of loyalty to his father. Mabel Hubbard herself resented being part of the deal; after prompting from her mother, she consented to Bell's proposal of marriage. Bell did promise Hubbard that he would work four days a week, from 9:00 a.m. until 2:00 p.m., on nothing but telegraphy, but it was a promise he was not able to keep. A training class for teachers of deaf students at Boston University was so heavily enrolled that it made heavy demands on his schedule. This, added to Bell's lifelong habit of doing his most creative work late at night, made his pledge to Hubbard unrealistic. Fortunately, Hubbard did not press the issue. If he had, society may have had to wait for someone else to invent the telephone, and Hubbard would never have made the fortune he did as a result of the invention.

By 1874, Bell had become increasingly interested in acoustical research. He was particularly fascinated with the manometric flame, a French invention that used a gas flame and a set of mirrors to give visual representations of actual sounds. Each sound resulted in a different pattern (i.e., a different shape of the flame). Bell immediately saw an application for teaching speech to deaf youngsters: A teacher might show a student what a sound was supposed to look like and then help the student to repeat the same sound.

Some researchers have stated that Bell's work with the manometric flame led directly to his invention of the telephone. This is incorrect— another myth surrounding the history of the telephone. It would, however, be accurate to state that Bell's enthusiasm for the device was fired by his interest in deafness, and that this experimentation greatly contributed to Bell's evolution as an inventor.

Bell's research in acoustics went far beyond the manometric flame. By 1876 his work on what was to become the telephone had attracted the attention of scientists and inventors. In May of that year Bell presented his work before the American Academy of Arts and Sciences, where it was received with enthusiasm. He had not as yet developed the telephone as we know it today, and while he was close, so too were several other people. Although Bell and his assistant, Thomas Watson, had their short, one-sided, but nonetheless historic conversation on March 10, 1876, actual transmission of speech was not perfected until a later date.

Another major event in Bell's life occurred during 1876 at the Centennial Exhibition in Philadelphia. His work with both Visible Speech and telephony found a place in the Massachusetts exhibit; his was one of the most widely discussed and reported exhibits at the fair. The judges were so impressed that they asked Bell to demonstrate his telephone apparatus an additional day. In characteristic style, Bell refused to stay in Philadelphia the extra day, but he arranged for an assistant to give the demonstration. He had to return to Boston in order to grade the exam papers of his deaf pupils.

Before the success of the telephone, Bell had constantly been concerned about money. While not destitute, he did not have the luxury of working full time on his inventions. His continuing work with deaf pupils was prompted by the need for a steady income as well as dedication to a cause. As Bell's reputation spread, lecturing offers increased, as did his financial resources. This security meant two things. First, it meant he could finally marry Mabel Hubbard. Even after she had consented to marry him, he had waited until he could provide her a more comfortable existence. The second thing his money did was allow him to follow his true leanings which, in addition to inventing, included the education of deaf children. In a letter to his wife he stated,

> Of one thing I become more sure every day, that my interest in the Deaf is to be a life-long thing with me. I see so much to be done, and so few to do it—so few qualified to do it. I shall never leave this work—and you must settle down to the conviction that whatever successes I may meet with in life—pecuniarily or otherwise—your teacher will always be known as a "teacher of deaf-mutes"—or interested in them.[7]

Bell's strong feelings in favor of day schools for deaf children have been noted. He was able to put these feelings into actual practice in England in 1877. A businessman from Greencock, Scotland, came to Bell to ask his assistance in starting a day school in that town. Bell not only organized the school but was also one of its first teachers. The school opened in 1878 with only three pupils, but Bell saw it as a pilot project. The school did much to whet his enthusiasm for establishing such schools in North America.

His next direct involvement with day schools came five years later, this time in Washington, D.C. He limited his class to six deaf pupils and arranged for a kindergarten class of hearing children on the first floor of the building. Bell hoped that the children would mix at certain times of the day, enhancing the deaf children's desire and ability to speak and read lips. In addition, a class for parents and friends of the deaf children was formed in order to help them support what the children had learned. Despite Bell's enthusiasm over the results of the school, it lasted only about two years. Problems in retaining a teacher plus heavy demands on Bell's time forced the school to close. Bell was so affected that he described his disposition to his wife as "shipwrecked."

The failure of this school did not dampen Bell's enthusiasm for day schools. He continued to speak out in their favor at every opportunity. He was, however, always careful to support them as an additional learning environment and not as a replacement for boarding schools. Some of the residential schools, especially the oral ones, offered excellent speech training. More importantly, residential schools and their supporters had political power. Bell correctly saw that if his campaign for day schools was seen as an attempt to replace residential schools, the likelihood of success would be greatly reduced. He wisely chose coexistence with residential schools, at times visiting them and even making occasional financial contributions.

The biggest roadblock to day schools for deaf students was the unwillingness of state governments to pay for them. In the early 1880s states supported only residential schools; if a family wished to send a child to a day school, it was forced to pay the tuition itself. Wisconsin led the way in state support for day schools. The state legislature there acted after years of lobbying by a group of concerned parents and citizens, and after hearing testimony from A. G. Bell. Wisconsin's system of schools grew rapidly, and in time, other states launched similar efforts. Bell was frequently called upon for support. Thus, while his own school was short-lived, the day school movement flourished. Bell described it as "the most important movement of the century for the benefit of the deaf."[8]

Despite Bell's attempts to separate the day school movement from the oral/combined debate, the two were eventually linked. This was inevitable; the majority of residential schools used sign language, while a desire for oral education fueled the day school movement. Residential schools, it was thought, did not offer a proper environment for oral education. They provided only a minimal amount of interaction between the deaf students and the hearing members of the community. North American residential schools began with a manual emphasis as a result of Thomas Hopkins Gallaudet's influence. Like residential schools of all types, these schools had a reputation for being conservative and slow to change. They truly earned this reputation by their unwillingness to add instruction in speech even after convincing evidence showed its desirability. The active support of a few sign language proponents, most notably Edward Miner Gallaudet, was required to convince these schools to attend to speech instruction.

While Bell never became fabulously wealthy from his inventions, his assets did approach one million dollars at one point—a substantial sum by nineteenth century standards. Not only did this wealth free Bell to explore areas of his choosing, it also allowed him to financially support individuals, organizations, and causes. For example, in 1886 he and a number of associates sold their rights to some patents relating to the phonograph. This transaction netted Bell more than $100,000. He used the money to establish what eventually was called the Volta Bureau, an organization supporting research and dissemination of information regarding deafness. In 1890, in the midst of hostilities with Gallaudet and the combined movement, Bell also gave $25,000 to found the American Association for the Promotion of the Teaching of Speech to the Deaf (AAPTSD). This organization still exists, though its name was changed in 1956 to, not surprisingly, the Alexander Graham Bell Association for the Deaf. This organization, through its meetings, lobbying efforts, and journal (the *Volta Review*), stands at the center of the oral movement in the United States.

One additional activity of Bell's related to deafness requires mention, though it did not involve him as a teacher, benefactor, or promoter. In 1887 an Alabama newspaper editor brought his daughter to see Bell. The girl was both deaf and blind, and her father had almost given up hope of finding a competent teacher for her. During the course of their interview, Bell did his best to communicate with the six-year-old child. While whole words were not exchanged, feelings apparently were. Describing this encounter eighteen years later, Helen Keller called it "the door through which I should pass from darkness into light."[9] Through Bell, inquiries were made of other professionals in the field, leading to the recruitment of Annie Sullivan as Keller's teacher.

Educational Philosophy

For some, integration was just one of many desired outcomes of education for deaf children. For Bell, however, integration was not one of many goals, or even among the most important; it was the main purpose of education. He rarely looked at the issue through the eyes of the individual; instead he took a broader, social view. Normal society, Bell maintained, consisted of people who could speak and hear and make use of the English language. The job of educators, therefore, was to prepare deaf children to make their way in that world by being able to communicate in English by speaking and reading lips (speechreading).

Society was clearly uppermost in Bell's mind when he defined his philosophy of education for deaf students.

> The great object of the education of the deaf is to enable them to communicate readily and easily with hearing persons, or rather to render intercommunication between the deaf and the hearing easy and certain. That is what is meant by "restoring the deaf to society."[10]

Once this philosophy was understood and accepted, it then followed that "the whole question . . . of education of the deaf is the question of language teaching. They must be taught to communicate readily and freely by means of the language in common use among the people in whose midst they live."[11]

Bell's opposition to sign language was based on the importance he attached to standard English. This, to him, was the key to successful integration. If a student could communicate only in sign language, he or she would never be able to integrate. This is not to say, however, that Bell rejected all forms of manual communication. Not only did he favor the use of fingerspelling with young children, but he complained that some teachers were actually too oral.

> I have no hesitation in saying that the attempt to carry on the general education of young children who are deaf from infancy by means of articulation and speechreading alone, without the habitual use of English in a more clearly visible form [manual alphabet], would tend to retard their mental development. . . . There is a tendency among teachers of articulation to rely too much upon the general intelligibility of their speech.[12]

In addition, Bell accepted the use of nonformalized gestures.

> I think that natural actions and gestures are of great utility in the instruction of the Deaf, when used as hearing people employ them, as accompaniments of English words, to emphasize and reinforce their meaning.... There are no teachers in existence who do not use them.[13]

Bell did feel that formalized gestures were harmful, especially the sign language developed in France by the Abbé de l'Epée. This was the sign language used, in much revised form, by the U.S. deaf population. Some educators, including E. M. Gallaudet, claimed that this sign language was the natural language of deaf people. Bell disagreed.

> The proposition that the sign language is the only language that is natural to congenitally deaf children is like the proposition that the English language is the only language that is natural to hearing children. It is natural only in the same sense that English is natural to an American child. It is the language of the people by whom he is surrounded.[14]

The adult deaf population did not take kindly to Bell's opposition to sign language. Interestingly, he actually admired signs from an aesthetic point of view, while maintaining that their use could greatly harm young children.

> I heartily agree with all that experienced teachers of the deaf have urged concerning the beauty and great interest of this gesture language. ... You may ask why it is that with my high appreciation of this language, as a language, I should advocate its entire abolition in our institutions for the deaf.

> I admit ... the ease with which a deaf child acquires this language and its perfect adaptability for the purpose of developing his mind; but after all it is not the language of the millions of people among whom his lot in life is cast.[15]

Thus, it is clear that Bell not only accepted the beauty of the language—he even accepted it for the purpose of developing the mind. Many oralists today claim that sign language is inferior to standard

English in many ways and that its use would work against the development of cognitive skills. This was never a concern of Bell's. For him, one thing was of paramount importance—integration. Sign language was an impediment to integration. For that reason, and that reason only, Bell opposed it.

The possibility that children might not be able to acquire oral skills, even in the best of programs, seemed never to occur to Bell. His total confidence in the oral system appears naive when read with today's knowledge and experience. In 1884, Bell wrote, "It is not generally known that the experimental stage has passed and that *all deaf-mutes can be taught intelligible speech* [italics added]."[16] He held a similar belief regarding speechreading skills: "With all who are deaf from infancy, we can certainly achieve . . . results [in speech-reading], if only we can give them a sufficient knowledge of our language at least in its written form."[17]

Unfortunately, history has not borne out Bell's confidence in the oral approach. All deaf children do not acquire intelligible speech. Oralists today know this, but that does not stop them from sharing Bell's intense conviction that it must be done, or at least attempted.

Most oralists today share Bell's aversion to sign language and would probably agree with his opinion that, if signing has any use at all, it is

> as a means of reaching and benefitting adults who are unable to communicate with the hearing world. But this field of usefulness lies beyond our province as instructors of the young. . . . The adults referred to represent our failures. Let us have as few of them as we possibly can.[18]

Labeling a person a *failure* because he or she uses sign language instead of standard English might seem harsh to some, as it obviously did to the adult deaf population in the 1890s. To them, attempts to eliminate sign language were tantamount to stripping them of their identity, their community, and their culture. They hated Bell for it. Bell lamented his poor standing within the deaf community, but his convictions were never shaken. He worked hard and effectively to promote the cause of oralism in the United States and abroad, and when the need arose for someone to square off against Edward Miner Gallaudet, Bell did not hesitate to step forward.

THREE

Edward Miner Gallaudet, 1857

A Lifelong Signer

U NLIKE A. G. Bell, who involved himself with many diverse activities, Edward Miner (E. M.) Gallaudet spent his entire life working with deaf people. This work was carried out almost exclusively in one place—the National Deaf-Mute College, which was renamed Gallaudet College (and now, University) in honor of his father, Thomas Hopkins Gallaudet. While their stories are different, there are numerous similarities between Gallaudet and Bell, the most important of which was their commitment to the goal of improving education for deaf students.

Early Influences

As was the case with Bell, Edward Gallaudet's mother was deaf. Unlike Eliza Bell though, Sophia Gallaudet had no usable hearing, and she had unintelligible speech. She depended on sign language to communicate, and her success in doing so strongly influenced her son's opinions on communication methodologies. She clearly affected not only his choice of communication method but his entire attitude toward deafness. In his first address as president of the National Deaf-Mute College in 1864, he stated,

> Dr. Gallaudet [his father] gave to the world the most convincing proof of his belief that the deaf and dumb could, through education, be made the social and intellectual equals of those possessed of all their faculties, by taking one of his own pupils as his wife.[1]

Thomas Hopkins Gallaudet played a crucial role in the establishment of the first school for deaf students in the United States. He headed the American Asylum for the Deaf and Dumb for thirteen years, beginning in 1817. By the time Edward was born in 1837, his father had retired from the school and was serving as the chaplain of the Hartford County Prison. The elder Gallaudet was a strong-willed, authoritarian man; an ordained minister who taught his children to both love and fear God. He made sure that his son studied every day, but never for more than three hours, since he believed that to become a complete person one would have to learn from life as well as from books.

E. M. Gallaudet was only twelve years old when his father first broached the idea of a career in deafness. As he later recalled,

> When I became a High School boy my father began to talk with me as to my future career, and I remember as though it were yesterday the occasion when he suggested that perhaps I might like to take up the work which had engaged the energies of his early manhood. He spoke at some length of the joy he had in doing what he believed was his Master's work . . . and said he believed I would never be sorry if I carried out his suggestion.[2]

After listening to his father, Edward replied that he wanted to make a lot of money in his lifetime and therefore wanted a career in business. The choice was taken out of his hands when his father died in 1851. Family finances were such that the fourteen-year-old Edward immediately had to find a job, which he did, as a clerk in a Hartford bank. Finding this job boring he reconsidered the idea of going to college and enrolled as a junior at Trinity College. In order to pay his way, he became a part-time teacher at the American Asylum. He was able to obtain the position through his family ties and his knowledge of sign language. This was Gallaudet's first actual involvement in the education of deaf children. Despite a total lack of formal training as a teacher, he did well.

The director of the American Asylum offered Gallaudet a full-time teaching job once he finished college, but Gallaudet was hesitant. His sense of adventure and desire for financial success conflicted with his need to live a purposeful life.

During this period of indecision, Gallaudet wrote in his diary that

> the temptations that assail me are many and great. Ambition whispers "Make for yourself a name." Mammon says "Labor for riches." The World says "Life is short, make the most of its pleasures." Oh God, let not these prevail against me.[3]

Choosing a Profession

For a while Gallaudet thought he wanted to become a minister and travel to the "untamed West" as an itinerant preacher. After graduation from Trinity, however, he decided not to make such a decision so early in life. He decided instead to go to China to establish a school for deaf students under the auspices of the American Board of Commissioners for Foreign Missions. However, a lack of money, and possibly a lack of commitment, prevented him from going; instead he accepted the position as a teacher at the American Asylum.

It is interesting to see how Gallaudet tried to satisfy both the missionary and the adventurous spirits within him at the same time. When his youthful plans failed to materialize, he gave up on adventure and decided to teach. Unbeknownst to him, there was plenty of adventure ahead.

About a year later, Gallaudet received an offer to become the superintendent of the new Columbia Institution for the Instruction of the Deaf and Dumb and the Blind in Washington, D.C. The offer was tendered by the school's organizer, Amos Kendall. As Gardiner Greene Hubbard was to Bell, Kendall was to Gallaudet. Kendall had made a great deal of money in telegraphy by joining forces with Samuel Morse in the 1840s. When Congress refused to grant Morse the money he needed to extend telegraph service from Baltimore to New York, he hired Kendall to be his business manager. Kendall was able to fund the project through private channels, eventually making fortunes for both himself and Morse. Thus, not only were Kendall and Hubbard mentors for Gallaudet and Bell, respectively; they were both successful telegraph promoters as well.

As a man of wealth, Kendall was able to bankroll worthy projects. One such project was a small school for deaf children in Washington, D.C. However, it happened that the man who had approached Kendall with the idea for a school did not have the best interests of the children in mind. He was in it for the money, and he reportedly mistreated the students. Once Kendall discovered this, he fired him, and organized a committee of Washingtonians to search for a successor. The committee also petitioned Congress to fund the school. Once the funding was secured, Gallaudet was asked to be superintendent.

In his initial interview with Kendall, Gallaudet expressed interest in the position as well as his desire to eventually expand the school into a college. Gallaudet thought the Washington school was perfect for such expansion. Its charter permitted attendance by children from any of the states and this, added to the location in the nation's capital, made it an ideal embryo for a national college for the deaf. No such college existed at the time, and Kendall gladly embraced Gallaudet's vision of the future.

By June of 1857 Gallaudet had moved his belongings from Hartford to Washington. After considerable anxiety, he had decided on a life of working with deaf students. His life in Washington and his position as superintendent at the Columbia Institution occupied him for the next 54 years, just 6 years short of his death.

The school that Gallaudet administered had nine deaf and five blind pupils in its first year, all of them boys. In addition, there were three assistants for Gallaudet, a matron, and an assistant matron. One of Kendall's conditions for Gallaudet's employment was that Gallaudet's mother accompany him to Washington to take on the job of matron. This appealed to the new superintendent and to the fourteen children who came to live on Kendall Green, as the campus eventually was called. Sophia Gallaudet and her assistant were the only women associated with the school, and the fact that she was deaf must have been a comfort to the children.

Gallaudet's mother must also have been a comfort to the school's board of directors, who were not happy having an unmarried man as superintendent. When Gallaudet married in 1858, it seemed less like a union of love than an act of expediency. Jane Fessenden Gallaudet was also from Hartford; she and Edward had known each other since childhood. Gallaudet's diary gives a good indication of the lack of depth of their relationship. He wrote that he married because he felt obliged to satisfy critics of his marital status. While his marriage satisfied the board, it is questionable whether it satisfied either partner. The Gallaudets' eight-year-marriage ended when Mrs. Gallaudet died in 1866. Less than one month later, Gallaudet wrote in his diary that the year had been an eventful one: "And so the old year is going—1866! Thou hast been an eventful year to me. A year of release! My heart fairly leaps within me as I think from what fetters I am loosed. Now I can live!"[4] This diary entry is bizarre, to say the least, coming so soon after Jane Fessenden's death.

Becoming a Leader

Amos Kendall had taken a chance in hiring Gallaudet as superintendent. Gallaudet was young, inexperienced, and untrained for the job. Yet, it is unlikely that Kendall ever had misgivings about the choice. Under Gallaudet's direction the school flourished. The student body and faculty grew, and in 1864 the school expanded to include the college. It was then, and still is, the only liberal arts college in the world with a deaf undergraduate student body. At the time, it was the only place in the world that offered postsecondary education to deaf students.

Gallaudet's success can be attributed mainly to his political expertise. The school was supported by federal funds, so every year Gallaudet had to go before Congress to acquire the necessary funding. Every time the school wished to build a new building, or raise salaries, or expand in any way, Congress had to be persuaded. This task was never easy, but Gallaudet's perseverance and skill in lobbying legislators resulted in far more victories than defeats. A student at the college noted Gallaudet's technique.

> It has been told that whenever the late Dr. E. M. Gallaudet was to appear before the Committee on Appropriations he used to take pains to dress himself very neatly. He would put on his best clothes after having been shaved by his barber, had a haircut and his shoes shined and finally squirted with perfume and then he was ready to appear

before the Committee. He used to have a team of horses drive him in a shiny elaborate carriage by his own coachman to the capitol. There he would alight from his carriage with great dignity and assisted by his coachman he would walk up to the front door.

Dr. Gallaudet would get up before the Committee when it was his turn, and make a graceful bow to all the members, and then in a clear cultured voice explain the needs of the college, its need for expansion, the number of deaf young men and women. . . . Whenever he was asked any questions he would always answer them very politely, and should he be the butt of a joke by a congressman who had an abundant sense of humor, he would always laugh with them and prove that he was a good fellow. . . . The meeting always ended with Dr. Gallaudet in his cutaway suit, shined shoes, immaculate white linen, with graceful gestures bowing right and left as he walked backwards to the door with a smile until he had disappeared through the door—a gentleman to the manner [sic] born.[5]

In his third month on the job, the school's board of directors assigned Gallaudet the task of planning an expansion of the institution. They envisaged the student body growing to fifty and needed buildings and teachers for them. A demonstration was arranged in order to gain support in Congress. Legislators visited the school, toured the classrooms, and had conversations with the children themselves. Newspaper writers and the leading citizens of Washington also participated, and their reactions to the demonstration were positive. So too was the vote of Congress. Gallaudet was wise in using his students to gain sympathy for the school. Gallaudet often used this technique of bringing policymakers face to face with the children with much success. It is a technique still used successfully by schools for handicapped children. While legislators can easily reject written requests, the outcome tends to be different when the children themselves plead the case.

Gallaudet made a practice of studying the political situation, identifying the most powerful people, and then cultivating their friendship and support for the school. One of his strongest supporters was Thaddeus Stevens, the House majority leader and chair of the Ways and Means Committee. Stevens controlled the pursestrings of the House, and he was on record as a friend of education. Gallaudet initiated their relationship by inviting Stevens to visit the school. As expected, once the congressman saw the school and the students, he became an immediate friend and supporter. This friendship resulted in passage of the necessary legislation to construct dormitories and other buildings on the campus once the college department was approved in 1864. It also helped Gallaudet's successful effort to have the blind children relocated to another institution; this action created a school whose sole purpose was to educate deaf students.

Though Gallaudet was usually successful in obtaining funding from Congress, the task was not always easy. One case in particular illustrates the difficulty he often encountered. The confrontation occurred in 1868 with Congressman Elihu Washburne of Illinois. Washburne's main objection stemmed from his belief that the federal government should not be supporting a school for deaf students. This responsibility, he claimed, should be shouldered by the individual states. He argued this view in a number of ways: Government money was being appropriated, but the power to spend it was in the hands of a private corporation; government money had been used to pay for land and buildings, but the title for this property was in the hands of that same corporation. Friends of the institute, led by Rufus Spalding of Ohio, drafted legislation to (a) prohibit the corporation from selling property without congressional authorization and (b) require that two representatives and one senator sit on the institution's board. Washburne was unappeased; he proposed that the number of students at the school be reduced, that the power of the superintendent be diluted, and that the title for all the school's property be transferred to the federal government.

At this point Gallaudet entered into the fray. Passage of Spalding's saving legislation was uncertain due to lack of support in the House-Senate Conference Committee. Four votes were needed for passage, two from each chamber. The pro-Gallaudet forces were one vote shy on the House side. Gallaudet invited Washburne to visit the school, but the fish didn't take the bait. Washburne knew that once he had seen the students, it would be difficult to carry on the fight against the school. Gallaudet then went to speak with another House member, Samuel Marshall. Armed with a letter of support from Amos Kendall, Gallaudet did his best to convince Marshall to vote with Spalding on the conference committee report. Gallaudet's powers of persuasion, coupled with Kendall's considerable prestige in the political arena, had the desired effect on Marshall. Despite all-out efforts by Washburne, Marshall cast the deciding vote in favor of the institution.

Washburne's efforts to limit the school's size and its yearly appropriation from Congress continued with little result. Gallaudet's knowledge of the workings of Congress, his skill in cultivating policymakers, and his sense of public perceptions of the very real need to support a school for deaf students, resulted in an almost unbroken string of legislative successes. In addition, Gallaudet was adept at securing advantages for the school from the private sector. When the college department was first established, he personally secured pledges of thousands of dollars that were used for scholarships. Even during the Civil War, when Union troops were bivouacked on the campus, Gallaudet made the best of things. The troops required fresh water, which in turn necessitated the installation of a special pipe from the campus to the Potomac River. Gallaudet ensured that the pipe would supply the school with fresh water long after the war was over, thereby saving the school thousands of dollars.

Gallaudet's skills as an administrator and fundraiser were considerable, but something else played an important part in his rise to leadership. Within the field of deaf education, no name carried greater prestige, commanded more respect, or invoked greater awe than did the name Gallaudet. Thomas Hopkins Gallaudet was the George Washington of his field, the *father* of education of the deaf in the United States. Streets were named for him, monuments were erected in his memory, and in 1895 the National Deaf-Mute College was renamed in his honor. There is little doubt that E. M. Gallaudet's family connection was the main reason behind Kendall's original offer of employment. He had done little to distinguish himself up until that time. It is also likely that his name, in addition to his position at the Columbia Institution, gave him the credibility necessary to emerge as a spokesperson for others within his field. However, to attribute Gallaudet's rise in the profession solely to his family connection would be a mistake. While this may have given him the opportunity to excel, it was through his own actions that he achieved a lasting reputation as an educational leader. His well-earned reputation was firmly established after his 1867 trip to Europe.

The Visit to Europe

The 1860s marked the emergence of the oral movement in the United States. The Clarke and Lexington schools were receiving much attention for their oral approaches and their adoption of techniques already used widely in Europe. In addition, a report written by Horace Mann and Samuel Howe twenty years earlier, which described their observations at European oral schools, also began receiving attention. The report praised oral methods and recommended their adoption in the United States. In 1867 the Massachusetts legislature released a report that criticized the lack of articulation training in schools for deaf students. In response to this report and the growing support for oralism, Gallaudet asked his board of directors for permission to make his own trip to Europe. The board granted permission and directed him to examine schools on the Continent and in Great Britain.

During his trip he visited schools of all kinds, observed classes, spoke with teachers and students, and took copious notes. These notes record that many instructors, even at the oral schools, had a low opinion of oral methods. It is difficult to determine the actual causes of these opinions. The director of one school in Belgium admitted that he believed articulation training was dangerous for children and that it did harm to their lungs. Besides, he said, most parents requested that speech not be taught, due to the "strange noises" the children made as a result of such training. There were also times when Gallaudet was impressed with what he saw of oral methods; he did not allow his manual background to blind him to the possibilities they held.

Gallaudet's trip and his subsequent report had significant influence on all schools for deaf students in the United States. In addition to describing his observations and interviews, he listed specific recommendations. The most important of these was that "instruction in artificial speech and lipreading be entered upon as early as possible," and that such instruction should be continued until "it plainly appears that success is unlikely to crown their efforts."[6] In addition, Gallaudet recommended that schools begin accepting students at an earlier age, increase the number of years of instruction, and hire additional personnel. Regarding the last point, he asked his board to consider the establishment of a normal department to train the additional teachers required to provide these services.

This 1867 report is generally credited with effecting the changeover from manual to combined education in U.S. schools for deaf children. Despite the mixed results of oral education that he observed in Europe, Gallaudet was convinced that some children could indeed benefit from speech training. He felt that it would be unfair to children to deprive them of at least the opportunity to learn oral skills. He followed his words with action; by hiring articulation teachers at his school, he set an example that most manual schools eventually copied. Gallaudet showed that he was willing to change his beliefs and his practices if he thought it in the students' best interests. He also demonstrated his belief that one method was not best for all children and that the individual needs of the children were of primary importance; therefore, any method that might assist a child to communicate should be accepted and developed, including speech.

Despite the surge of interest in oral education and the increasing number of oral schools in the 1860s, manualists were initially slow to respond to calls for speech instruction in their schools. Until Gallaudet's report, the two sides were so polarized that little compromise seemed possible. Movement came only after Gallaudet, an established supporter of sign language, raised the need for speech. Gallaudet's move was courageous, prompting some to label him a traitor to the cause of sign language. Sometimes, though, it takes a person from the opposite camp, whose credentials and support are above question, to make the first move. Gallaudet's actions were seen as signs of strength, not weakness, and so he gained the support of a significant number of people.

Gallaudet's stance established him as the leader of the combined movement, a role that led him into conflict with oralists. The first direct instance of conflict occurred as the result of the 1868 conference of principals of schools for deaf students. Gallaudet himself organized this conference, and his personal agenda included convincing manual schools to include speech training. Among the other topics planned for discussion was the articulation controversy. Gallaudet was afraid that the meeting would degenerate into a debate between oralists and manualists, which would then result in no movement by either side. In a tactical move of questionable wisdom, Gallaudet excluded leaders of oral schools from this meeting. When the 1868 Conference of Principals convened in Washington, only sign language proponents attended.

Gallaudet used a technicality to exclude the oralists: since none of the newly established oral schools actually had principals, and since the conference did not include head teachers or members of boards of directors, the exclusion of oralists was justified. Unofficially, Gallaudet felt that the presence of oralists would doom the conference to failure. It was their avowed purpose, he felt, to discredit manual communication, and he saw no reason to include them. As a result of the conference, a number of principals who had formerly been opposed to speech instruction changed their minds and decided to offer it at their schools. Gallaudet was almost certainly correct in assuming that such compromises would not have occurred in an adversarial setting. The long-term effects, however, were serious. Oral educators viewed the conference, and their exclusion, as an early round in a head-to-head struggle for dominance in the field of deaf education. While manual schools were becoming combined in their approach, reconciliation between the oral and manual camps took a step backward.

Over the next decade, the argument continued in a low-key fashion. The number of oral schools increased and there was little change in the number of schools using sign language. Gradually, the vast majority of programs followed Gallaudet's lead and changed from manualism to combined techniques. In 1880, though, the pendulum took a swing toward oralism, despite Gallaudet's best efforts to prevent it. The setting was the International Convention of Instructors of the Deaf, in Milan, Italy. After hearing testimony on both sides of the communication issue, the convention voted overwhelmingly to support oral education. The effect of this vote was substantial both in Europe and the United States. It gave the oral movement considerable credibility and infused its leaders with an almost messianic belief in the rightness of their approach.

Gallaudet described the Milan conference as a "stacked deck" in favor of oralism. He pointed out that more than half the delegates were Italian and that for years the Italians had been trying to establish oralism as the only way to teach deaf children. He felt the vote for oralism was preordained. In addition, Gallaudet noted that Italy had the abundant resources to hire twice as many teachers as the United States. Despite Gallaudet's rebuttal, U.S. oralists made good use of the conference's decision, correctly pointing to it as the pivotal incident in the growth of the oral movement in the United States.

Educational Philosophy

Gallaudet cared deeply about deaf people and always looked to what he perceived as their best interests. He was one of the first to study the adult deaf population in order to determine the best ways of educating children. And while he rarely shared his emotions with others, his diary reveals some of his personal and deeply held beliefs. Shortly after the Confederate surrender in 1865, Gallaudet took a boat trip to Charlestown to watch the flag raising at Fort Sumter. During the trip he visited the homes and schools of ex-slaves. He described the experience as "sickening, to one who believes as I do in the right pertaining to every human being to better his condition if he has within him the power and desire to do so."[7]

Oralists had claimed that proponents of sign language knowingly condemned deaf people to limited lives bound by the walls of communication that sign language imposed. It seems clear that, to Gallaudet, it was the breaking down of those walls that was important. While his methods can be doubted, his intent is certainly beyond question.

Shortly after the establishment of oral schools in New York and Massachusetts, the communication issue caught fire. In 1868, Edward Gallaudet took a stand in favor of the combined approach—an approach that included speech instruction as well as sign language. His insistence on looking at both sides of the issue and his refusal to blindly reject all oral arguments caused some to label him as a traitor to the philosophical ideals of his late father. He countered such criticism by stating that he would

> offer no apology for calling attention to those defects his friendly eye sees in the practical workings of a system to the upbuilding and perfecting of which he has devoted the best years of his life; a system that is endeared to him by every consideration of filial respect.[8]

Throughout his career, Gallaudet believed that all sides of an issue deserved at least a fair hearing. In that spirit, he asked his colleagues,

> What then is the part of wisdom for us? To rest on the laurels of the past ... to ignore the good that is to be found in the opposing system ... to allow a penny wise, pound foolish notion of sparing expense, to economize the life out of our whole work?

> No! a thousand times. No! to all these damaging suggestions. We will rather address ourselves seriously to the task of ascertaining wherein improvements in our work are possible, and then use all means in our power to realize these improvements.[9]

It is an interesting and little-known fact that Gallaudet, though he championed the use of sign language against those who would eliminate it entirely, was aware that the indiscriminate use of signs could be a problem. As early as 1868, long before his battles with Bell, Gallaudet wrote,

> The language of signs in its present state of development furnishes so easy and exact and beautiful a means of communication between teacher and pupil, that the temptation is strong to use it to an extent which may operate unfavorably upon the pupil . . . .
>
> Teachers and officers use signs far too freely; pupils are allowed to use them long after they might employ the finger alphabet in many of their communications . . . .
>
> Their great object is to acquire a means of communicating accurately with the world in general. The failure to do this, manifest in too many of the graduates of our institutions, stands forth as the gravest practical defect of our system.[10]

Despite the fact that Gallaudet criticized certain aspects of the sign language system and agreed with oralists that signs could ultimately be destructive, he stopped far short of calling for the abandonment of signs. He suggested instead that signs be seen as a means to an end, not an end unto themselves.

There has long been a school of thought insisting that integration of deaf with hearing children is irrelevant and should not be a major objective of education of the deaf. Instead, development of the individual's own abilities is considered the great object of education. Integration, to this group, is an acceptable, even positive happenstance, but by no means is it the only desirable outcome. While Gallaudet was certainly in tune with this emphasis on individual development, he nevertheless put great value on integration. He feared that excessive use of sign language might retard integration.

In 1870, his loyalty was again called into question. Speaking before a convention of educators in Indianapolis, Gallaudet again stated that signs might be used to excess. He called sign language a "dangerous thing" when used to excess. This speech created such negative public opinion among manualists that he felt the need to reply to his critics.

He first addressed the loyalty issue in an article titled "Is the Sign Language Used to Excess in Teaching Deaf-Mutes?."

> In advocating the use of the sign language, at almost every stage of progress in the training of a deaf-mute, the writer would be counted as second to none; in acknowledging the force, clearness and beauty of expression possible in this language, he would be ranked among its most enthusiastic admirers;... he would at the same time, maintain, with all respect to those of a contrary opinion, that in the abuse of signs, and by this is meant their excessive use, may be found one of the gravest defects under which our national system of teaching the deaf is laboring.[11]

By maintaining such an open-minded position on the question of methods, Gallaudet separated himself from those whose goals were less educational than political. The reputation he gained was to serve him well some years later when he became the primary spokesperson for the combined method in debates with A. G. Bell. One must not be misled, however, by his attitude toward methods. As even-handed as he appeared, he made no secret regarding his sympathies on the communication issue. He was a proponent of signs and was fond of quoting his father's statement on signing: "So far as motions or actions addressed to the sense are concerned, this language ... is superior in accuracy and force of delineation to that in which words spelt of the fingers, spoken, written or printed, are employed."[12]

Edward Gallaudet admitted that the assertion of the superiority of signs over words "may excite surprise at first thought," but he defended it. "Meanings attached to words are almost wholly arbitrary," he wrote, "while nearly every gesture used in sign language carries with it a plain suggestion of its meaning."[13]

While granting that oral methods might succeed for some in classroom settings, Gallaudet felt that oralists were

> utterly incapable of giving the deaf, either in school or after they have passed into adult years, the great comfort and benefit of public addresses. For it is through the use of the sign language alone that the deaf can enjoy lectures, sermons, or debates.[14]

This concern with communication in group settings was frequently voiced by Gallaudet, particularly as it applied to religion. In an 1895 newspaper interview, he said,

> It is worthy of remark, in balancing the advantages of the methods ... that very few of the orally-taught deaf can follow, understandingly, the utterances of an ordinary public speaker ... The claim, often made, that many can do this, is without foundation. Proof of this is afforded in the fact that the great majority of the graduates of the pure oral schools soon connect themselves with churches and classes where religious instruction is given in signs, speedily learning the language ... if indeed they have not already acquired it surreptitiously, as is very common.[15]

Oralists have argued that sign language should be abandoned because its use retards the development of speech. This point was debated throughout the nineteenth century, despite the fact that both sides had little factual proof. Gallaudet, not surprisingly, supported the sign language position.

> The very prevalent idea that, in order to secure the best results in speech with deaf children it is necessary to banish the sign language from their schools, is wholly without foundation either in philosophy or fact. Deaf children ... will not be hindered by a judicious use of the language offered them by nature, any more than the acquirement of German by an Englishman will be retarded if the teacher makes an occasional use of his mother tongue.[16]

The important words here are "the language offered them by nature." It was always Gallaudet's belief, as it was his father's and de l'Epée's, that sign language was the *natural* language of deaf people, as natural as standard English was for children in Britain or the United States. The objective of the oral method was communication in standard English, something Gallaudet considered artificial. In speeches and articles, he referred to it as the *artificial method*. Gallaudet felt that deaf children had a right to use their natural language, and he considered himself to be the champion of that right. This sense of conviction, added to his formidable skills and reputation, made him an effective proponent of the sign language movement.

F O U R

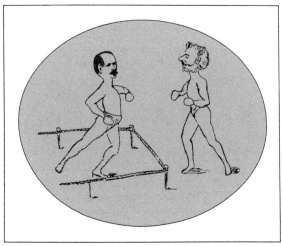

Cartoon from *The Silent Echo,* October 1, 1892, depicting
E. M. Gallaudet's and A. G. Bell's opposing views on
communication methods.

The Growing Rivalry

WHEN Gallaudet left Washington for his European tour of
schools in 1867, he went by way of Hartford and Boston. In
addition to seeing friends in Hartford, he hoped to score points
for sign language in Boston, which at that time was the center of support
for oralism. The Massachusetts state legislature previously had been
impressed by a demonstration of the oral skills of a number of deaf
children, including the young Mabel Hubbard. Gallaudet attempted to
counteract this demonstration with one of his own, using a student from
the college who had excellent speech and speechreading ability in addition
to manual skills. Gardiner Greene Hubbard, probably the initial contact
between Bell and Gallaudet, was Gallaudet's host in Boston. The two
got along well, despite their difference in communication preference.

During Gallaudet's visit, Hubbard gave a party for his guest. A
number of Harvard University professors attended, and so did Mabel
Hubbard and another orally taught deaf child, Jeanie Lippitt. Gallaudet

was impressed with the oral skills exhibited by the girls, but attributed their success to the fact that they probably had not become deaf until the age of four or five. He later noted that both girls came from wealthy families who were able to afford the best possible education. Wealth was a factor that Gallaudet often raised, arguing that the small class sizes and individual instruction required in oral programs were luxuries beyond the reach of the average family.

Gallaudet admired A. G. Bell's work so much that he offered Bell a professorship at the college in Washington in 1867. The offer came at a bad time for Bell, who was feeling pressure from Hubbard, his financial backer, to cut back on outside activities and concentrate fully on inventions. While Bell gave the offer serious consideration, he ultimately rejected it. The fact that the offer was made and considered, however, indicates that each man respected the other.

When Bell moved to Washington in 1878 he joined the Cosmos Club, of which Gallaudet was also a member. In 1880 Gallaudet's diary records their first private dinner, an event they repeated infrequently over the next few years in a climate of friendly rivalry. A Gallaudet diary entry in 1881 describes one such dinner as a "sparring match." Further evidence of the men's mutual admiration occurred in 1880 when the college, at Gallaudet's request, conferred an honorary Ph.D. upon Bell. It was the first of many such degrees that Bell received.

The gradual disintegration of the relationship between Bell and Gallaudet did not represent an actual falling out between the two men. Rather, it indicated the growing rift between oralists and combinists and the emergence of the two men as leaders of the opposing sides. Cordiality continued to be the order of the day, at least outwardly. But, as their friendly competition continued, the stakes got higher.

A public demonstration of their competitiveness occurred in 1881 at a convention of social scientists. Gallaudet had been invited to deliver a paper entitled "The Best Method of Educating the Deaf." He had given a copy of the paper to Bell and asked him to publicly sustain his (Gallaudet's) views. This Bell agreed to do. Gallaudet's presentation went as planned, but Bell's supposed affirmation three days later expressed only mixed support. He agreed with Gallaudet on some points and differed on others. Gallaudet later claimed that he had expected to receive such a response, but if he expected it, he did a poor job of preparing for it. When he asked the convention chairperson for a few minutes to reply to Bell, he was refused. By not requesting this time prior to the meeting, he allowed Bell to have the last word in the debate.

The next significant confrontation between them came at the 1884 Conference of Principals of Schools for the Deaf in Faribault, Minnesota. Gallaudet attended as a principal, and Bell came as one of fifty-three honorary members. This honorary group included teachers, directors, and other school officers, a group that Gallaudet had taken pains to exclude from the 1868 gathering (see chap. 3). The growing strength of the oral movement was much in evidence at the 1884 meeting. Communication methods were debated, with Gallaudet and Bell trading views in a forceful yet professional fashion.

By 1886, the Conference of American Instructors of the Deaf had passed a resolution calling for all schools for deaf students to offer speech instruction. It recommended that this instruction be terminated only when it was clear that the success attainable was so small that it no longer justified the effort. This resolution, when added to Gallaudet's earlier call for speech, should have settled the matter, but it did not. According to statistics compiled by oral advocates and undisputed by combinists, the number of students receiving speech instruction actually dropped between 1886 and 1887. This fact may have prompted Bell to write (with less tolerance than usual) to Gallaudet that, "I have hourly—daily—experience of [the value of speech] in my own home, and my heart bleeds for the speaking young men at the College who are placed under deaf teachers with deaf companions."[1] The letter further urged Gallaudet to stop the practice of hiring deaf teachers to teach deaf students.

Changes in educational methods were also occurring outside the United States. In 1886, Gallaudet was invited to speak before a royal commission in England that was investigating the various ways of educating deaf students. The commission was a follow-up to the Milan Conference of 1880, which had voted overwhelmingly to support oralism and had provided a major impetus to the oral movement in the United States. A number of the members of the royal commission had attended the Milan meeting, so Gallaudet was prepared for a cool reception. He testified for a day and spent another day answering questions from the commissioners; by the end of his testimony, he felt pleased that he had done so well in what he perceived to be a hostile setting.

Bell also testified before the commission, though not until two years later. Originally scheduled for one day of testimony, he actually testified through four days. Feeling that he had expressed an effective case for oral education, Bell had his testimony bound and distributed. Like Gallaudet, Bell thought that his views had been well received. He was so confident, in fact, that he asked Gallaudet's permission to publish the latter's testimony side-by-side with his own. Bell offered Gallaudet the opportunity to add

> anything you desire to say in way of comment upon my testimony. I cannot, of course, expect it to be all quite palatable to me—but what of that? Honest controversy never hurts truth—and that is what we are after—both of us—I am sure.[2]

Gallaudet rose to the challenge and consented to the arrangement. He took pains to assure Bell that his comments would indeed be *palatable:* "I do not think I shall say anything in the postscript that will disturb you seriously. We are seeking to arrive at the truth, and to use a little current slang, I think we shall both get there ultimately."[3]

Open hostilities finally broke out between Gallaudet and Bell over the issue of a normal school at Gallaudet College. Teacher training had captured Gallaudet's imagination when he first saw a normal school in Milan in 1867. In 1890, with the number of schools for deaf students increasing, a need arose for qualified teachers. Gallaudet saw his college as the logical place for a training program. The school's location, added to Gallaudet's extensive network of legislative connections, led him to believe that establishing such a program would present little difficulty. He had not reckoned, however, with Alexander Graham Bell.

Bell's views on a government-supported training school should have been well known to Gallaudet. In his testimony before the royal commission in London, Bell had said that he "would not advocate the establishment, by the government, of a special training school for the teachers of the deaf, for this reason, that it will tend to the perpetuation of some one method of instruction."[4] Bell did not object to a school's adherence to a single method of instruction. Indeed, he often spoke of the need for a normal school which, presumably, would adhere only to oral techniques. Rather, his objection was to state support for that school. Despite Bell's views, Gallaudet went to see him about the idea. He even invited Bell to lecture at the school after its establishment and understood Bell to say that he would accept this offer.

In Gallaudet's 1890 "Report to Congress" he asked for an additional $5,000 to establish a normal department at the college. He then began his usual lobbying efforts, meeting with members of the House Appropriations Committee to explain the purpose of the new department and the national need for it. However, in January of 1891 he learned that Bell had asked permission to address the Appropriations Committee to oppose the normal department. Gallaudet's diary entries at this time reflect his surprise and sense of betrayal at Bell's move. On January 24 he wrote, "I learned last night from General Cogswell that Graham Bell has asked for a hearing before the Approp. Com. to [disapprove of] our Normal School scheme. Shame!"[5]

A day later he wrote, "Prof. Fay [a College faculty member] kindly offered to see Prof. Bell this evening and let him know I felt aggrieved at his unfriendly attitude taken without any consultation with me."[6] This last comment shows that Gallaudet was upset for two reasons. First, he didn't appreciate any opposition to his plan. Second, he was particularly disturbed that Bell had not consulted with him before going public with his opposition. Gallaudet was not used to being questioned on policy issues, and he took Bell's move as a personal insult.

Was Gallaudet's plan for a normal school motivated by pedagogy or politics? It seems likely that the move, at least in part, was intended to fortify the combined system against the oral onslaught. Describing a meeting with Bell on January 26, Gallaudet wrote,

> I had an hour's talk with Prof. Bell this forenoon at his home, finding him much stirred at the prospect of our Normal School succeeding. I said a good deal to him—but I fear with little effect. He sees plainly that with both college and Normal School here, it would be hard work to make headway against such a citadel of the combined system.[7]

Bell's reasons for opposing the new department were a mix of the political and educational. He abhorred the idea of deaf teachers for deaf children because this guaranteed the deemphasis of articulation training. Gallaudet countered this criticism by verbally promising Bell that the oral method would be taught at the normal school and that no deaf students would be admitted into the teacher training classes.

Both men testified before the Appropriations Committee on the same day; Bell spoke first. He mentioned that oral schools supported themselves through tuition and private donations; he also said that government support should not be necessary for combined schools such as Gallaudet's. Then he stated his true fear—that the real purpose of the normal school was to train deaf teachers.

> The graduates of the collegiate department are of course deaf. This, therefore, is a proposition to train deaf persons to teach the deaf. I consider this a backward step, and not a step in advance. Instructors of the deaf, so far as possible, should be in full possession of all their faculties. . . .
>
> The percentage of deaf teachers employed has steadily decreased, and must decrease still further to a very great extent on account of the increasing attention paid to articulation teaching. . . .
>
> The employment of deaf teachers is absolutely detrimental to oral instruction, and the training school proposed by President Gallaudet should therefore not be supported by the United States.[8]

Bell recognized that the act before Congress did not specifically aim to train deaf teachers; also, in theory the program would be eclectic in its approach to communications methods. While this might be fine in theory, he stated, it would be impossible to implement effectively. The college was committed to combined methods and therefore could not be expected to give equal attention to oral methods.

> You might as well try to establish in connection with a Roman Catholic college, a national theological seminary in which all religions should be taught, the Roman Catholics to receive the money and agreeing to turn out Protestant ministers of the gospel as well as Roman Catholic priests.
>
> The national College is behind the age in the matter of oral teaching, and we can not trust to it to train teachers of the oral method.[9]

It is very important to remember that, prior to this testimony, Bell had received Gallaudet's verbal promise that the normal school would not accept deaf students. It is clear from Bell's testimony, however, that he did not believe Gallaudet. His words implied that, due to the combined environment at the college, oral methods would take second place, despite the best intentions of the faculty. Bell went even further in another statement to the committee.

> I observe ... that both the oral and sign methods will be taught. To oral teachers this seems a most extraordinary proposition. We must be pardoned for believing that the son of the introducer of the sign method will himself seek to propogate the sign language.[10]

Despite Bell's testimony, the committee voted to support Gallaudet and appropriate the money. The issue then moved to the Senate for the next battle. Gallaudet's diary reveals the toll that this fight was exacting on him.

> I think I came out ahead before the [Senate] Committee. We kept good natured and parted in a friendly way. I feel, however, a good deal aggrieved, personally, at the attitude taken by Bell .... The strain on my nervous system is severe—but I am bearing it, I think.[11]

Gallaudet's first setback came sometime after the House Appropriations Committee vote. He learned that in addition to approving the $5,000 for the normal school, the committee had deleted $3,000 for improvement of the grounds. This action had nothing to do with Bell; it was probably due to the general debate over funding for the school. No cuts had ever been made in this category of aid, and Gallaudet could not help but place the blame on Bell.

The next setback came during the fight for Senate approval of the appropriation. This time Bell's efforts to defeat Gallaudet's proposal were successful. Bell began by writing a scathing letter to Senator William Allison in opposition to the appropriation. Allison, besides being on the Senate Appropriations Committee, was a friend of the college. Bell's letter was essentially a rehash of his prior testimony in the House. He stated that oral education was better than combined education, and he urged a policy of nonintervention by the federal government. He felt that each method should stand or fall on its own merit, without the "artificial" support of federal money.

Bell knew that if the government suspended its support of schools for deaf students, oral schools would benefit. These schools were established after the creation of government-supported schools, and they depended on private donations and endowments. Bell himself was a frequent and generous benefactor. The older schools, those that used combined methods, had no network of private support. Some of them undoubtedly would have been forced to close without continued government assistance.

News of Bell's opposition spread throughout the field of deaf education and elicited a number of protests. J. R. Dobyns, the superintendent of a state school in Mississippi, wrote Bell,

> You have been greatly honored by all who are interested in education of the deaf. . . . I have felt that your course has been a blessing to the cause of the education of the deaf. . . .
>
> After all these years of earnest and faithful, but generous rivalry, I am indeed grieved that you have taken a step, the logical result of which is to build up the method which you advocate by tearing down the one which, for almost a century, has showered incalculable blessings upon the deaf in this country.[12]

Bell responded to this letter by saying that it was not his intent to "tear down" any one method. "All I ask," he wrote, "is to let the methods alone—let them be worked out by private enterprise and the fittest will survive."[13] But many people felt that Bell was trying to do away with sign language. Gallaudet's diary notation of February 16, 1891, is somewhat less polite than Dobyns's letter: "It is a pitiful spectacle— considering Bell—to see a man of naturally generous impulses, given over to partisan spite. Bell has sent a letter to Senator Allison, full of garbled statements and misrepresentations."[14] Three days after this entry, Bell gave a dinner for a friend, Dr. Gillett. Gallaudet, a mutual friend and colleague of Gillett's was also invited. Though no record exists of any conversation between the adversaries, Gallaudet wrote later that "I kicked, mentally, at accepting Bell's hospitality."[15]

Bell and Gallaudet's relationship eroded further when the Senate agreed with Bell and eliminated the $5,000 for the normal school from the college's budget. The decision shocked Gallaudet. He wrote, "Every day lowers Bell in my esteem."[16] He was particularly upset that Bell continued to assert that the normal school was designed to train deaf teachers of deaf students. In Gallaudet's view, Bell was calling him a liar; it appeared that Bell did not trust Gallaudet's verbal assurances that the school would not admit deaf students.

Bell's primary reason for rejecting Gallaudet's promise had nothing to do with Gallaudet or the communication debate. Bell distrusted all agreements, whether oral or written. His experiences when patenting the telephone had made him especially skeptical of verbal assurances.

The invention of the telephone was initially a mixed blessing for Bell and his family. While it ultimately made him wealthy, the road from invention to riches was anything but smooth. He spent months in court defending his work against numerous adversaries who claimed either that they had thought of the idea first or that Bell had stolen their ideas. Some of these encounters were with serious inventors and scientists; others involved schemers and swindlers. The experience was a bitter and sobering one for the young idealist—and he never forgot it. From that time on, Bell was careful to document everything, to shun verbal agreements, and to get everything in writing. Perhaps if Gallaudet had been aware of Bell's past experiences, he would have excused Bell's unwillingness to accept his word. As it was, however, he considered Bell's actions unprofessional and not befitting a gentleman.

Though the Senate sided with Bell by eliminating the appropriation for the normal school, it appears that Bell gave Gallaudet the opening he needed to establish the school. Much to his surprise, Gallaudet received a letter from Bell in which Bell reported that he had asked Henry Dawes, the senator from Massachusetts, to offer an amendment of $3,000 for the college to subsidize oral instruction. Bell's supporters explained this move as an act of charity by a man of principle, one who put educational issues above political infighting. However, others claimed that Bell's action was a response to growing pressure from legislators and educators. Gallaudet apparently shared this belief; he wrote in his diary that "Bell has heard from the 'back districts'."[17] Nevertheless, Gallaudet seized this opportunity and pushed for passage of the amendment, and Congress complied. Using the $3,000 and an appropriation by the college's board of directors, Gallaudet established a normal school. This move caught Bell by surprise, but it was perfectly legal. As Gallaudet had promised, the school accepted normally hearing students only and these students learned oral methods.

Gallaudet had won a victory of sorts. The normal school he established in 1891 is still one of the most respected teacher training departments in the field of education of deaf students. It would grieve Bell to know that a large number of deaf students are now enrolled in the program. He would, however, take comfort in the fact that other programs continue to practice his belief in oral methods.

This episode permanently and negatively affected the relationship between these two influential men. Despite his best efforts, Bell lost his fight to prevent the establishment of the normal school. In the process, he intimated that Gallaudet was a liar and that he could not be trusted. Indeed, after Gallaudet took advantage of the $3,000 to start the normal school, it seems likely that Bell felt vindicated in this belief. As for Gallaudet, his image as a dependable provider for his school was tarnished. More importantly, his attitude toward Bell shifted from respect to disdain. After a chance meeting between the two, Gallaudet wrote, "Met Bell at the Capitol today and was glad of a chance to be cool to him."[18]

Shortly after Congress had settled the appropriations matter, Gallaudet described the chain of events to James Welling, president of Columbian University (now George Washington University). Welling attributed Bell's actions to "the development of the millionaire spirit," and implied that men as rich as Bell were used to getting their way.[19] This opinion does Bell an injustice; it ignores motives that, at least in part, were altruistic. Both Bell and Gallaudet were willing to fight in order to prevail, and it was inevitable that their association would result in sparks. The normal school issue only provided the tinder for the fire.

Before leaving this episode, it is interesting to note the styles that Bell and Gallaudet exhibited during the fray. Gallaudet exemplified the savvy insider. He knew the key members of Congress and how to sway them. He lobbied the policymakers in their homes, their offices, and in Capitol Hill cloakrooms. Bell shirked such methods. When a friend suggested that he invite influential members of Congress to dinner he became furious, saying, "If the facts presented to these gentlemen do not convince them of the merits of this case, they can go to blazes!"[20] Nonetheless, he did write letters to enlist support among other oral educators. He also made personal appeals to Senators Washburne and Allison.

In one way, Bell was the victor. The Senate did vote to withhold the original appropriation for a normal school. By any civics book definition, that should have been the end of it. However, Gallaudet knew that only in civics books were rules cast in stone; in practice they could be bent or interpreted in creative ways. Thus he was able to absorb his loss in Congress and still establish the school. The victory was bittersweet, however; it prompted this entry in Gallaudet's diary:

> I experienced a profoundly thankful feeling this evening as I realized that my great struggle for the Normal School was over. Bell has made it hard for me, but Providence has helped me and I feel fresh and vigorous after the fight. My great regret is that I have to think so poorly of Bell.[21]

As future events were to show, Bell's opinion of Gallaudet was also low—and destined to go lower.

FIVE

Edward Miner Gallaudet, 1889

Irreconcilable Differences

THE fight over the normal school drove a permanent wedge between Bell and Gallaudet. During the period just after this traumatic incident, the two men exchanged numerous letters and messages. They each had the same goal—to convince the other that he had been treated unfairly, unprofessionally, and dishonestly. With the eyes of the deaf world upon them, they attempted to receive satisfaction from each other by outwardly expressing the desire to work together while inwardly jockeying for a position of ascendancy within the field of deaf education.

Each man felt that his honor had been questioned. Gallaudet had promised Bell that no deaf students would be admitted into the normal school. When Bell refused to believe it and testified publicly that deaf students would indeed enroll, Gallaudet felt Bell was calling him a liar. From Gallaudet's perspective, Bell was being dishonest by continuing to make the claim despite Gallaudet's assurances to the contrary.

This bickering was closely watched by Bell's and Gallaudet's colleagues. The actions of the two men, and the eventual outcome of their conflict, had an enormous impact on thousands of lives. It is fair to say, in fact, that the personal feud between Bell and Gallaudet had an impact equal to that of their more mature efforts in the areas of pedagogy and philanthropy.

A Question of Honor

Gallaudet's main complaint stemmed from Bell's testimony before Congress that the normal school would train deaf teachers. Bell's complaint stemmed from a speech Gallaudet made to a group of students at the National Deaf-Mute College. The speech, reproduced in the college publication *Companion* of March 7, 1891, was Gallaudet's version of the course of events connected with the legislative battle for the normal school. After blaming the unfavorable vote on Bell's interference, Gallaudet made a statement that stuck in Bell's craw.

> Bell was not satisfied with the muddle he had already made by meddling in affairs that did not concern him, and wrote letters to all the schools and institutions in the country, that were so worded as to misguide those not informed, and also contained several untruths, *that were untruths to his knowledge* [italics added].[1]

When these words were reproduced in the *Companion,* and gained widespread attention, Bell went into action. On March 16, 1891, he wrote to Gallaudet,

> Since I saw you in Philadelphia my attention has been directed to the enclosed cutting from the *Companion* of March 7th, 1891. Allow me to ask you whether it contains a true account of the remarks you made to the students of the college concerning me. I have, myself, so often been mis-quoted in the Deaf-Mute Journals—that I hope sincerely you have been incorrectly reported.[2]

The tone of Bell's letter was polite and friendly; it almost implied that Gallaudet could never have said the things quoted from his speech. However, a letter Bell wrote to his wife, Mabel, on the same day, indicated how serious Bell was about Gallaudet's speech.

I have just sent [the] letter to President Gallaudet which I trust may lead him to explain himself—without my taking any public action. Mr. Hubbard [Bell's father-in-law] says he has written or communicated with Sen. Dawes, suggesting that the Directors of the Institution—or Congress—make some investigation of the matter. I think however it is wise to find out first whether the statements are true. I feel very sorry for President Gallaudet for the mess he has brought himself into. I certainly do not feel it is right for me to pass by entirely un-noticed, such remarks as those he has been reported to have made.

I only hope that he has been misquoted. This letter will give him a chance to withdraw the remarks.[3]

Before Gallaudet replied to Bell, Mabel Bell wrote her husband. Her tone of moderation and support were characteristic of her reactions throughout the entire affair, and indeed, throughout her entire relationship with Bell.

I am very much pleased with your letter to Mr. Gallaudet. It is just exactly what it should be, to the point, dignified, and wasting not words. I wonder how it will be answered. But I hardly see why a Congressional investigation should be called for. Hasn't Congress something more important to do than to hear personal charges of this kind? It is however rather a different matter where the Directors of the College are concerned. If Mr. Gallaudet does not accept the loophole of escape you offer they should certainly be appealed to.[4]

Another day passed with no response from Gallaudet. In a note to his wife, Bell's resolve hardened.

Gallaudet hangs fire—no reply to my letter yet. I wrote as friendly a note as it was possible for me to send under the circumstances. If he will only respond like a gentleman—I won't harbor any ill-will against him. I have always treated him with courtesy and it is surely his duty to treat me in the same way. If he does not—I shall certainly ask for an investigation from his Board of Directors.[5]

Later that day (March 18) Gallaudet's reply finally reached Bell. Gallaudet knew the part of his speech that troubled Bell, and so came right to the point:

The most serious error [in the transcription of the speech] is found in the conclusion of the sentence I have taken the liberty of marking, "and also contained several untruths that were untruths to his knowledge."

What I did say was that after certain facts had been brought to your notice by me . . . you published statements . . . from which many important facts known to you were omitted.

I have, however, taken pains not to say anything to any person anywhere, as to your recent course, that could justly be considered at variance with the precepts of courtesy and fair dealing accepted by gentlemen. If reporters have represented me otherwise, I must appeal to your own eminently pertinent remark: "If you want to do a man justice, you should believe what a man says himself, rather than what people say he says."[6]

Like Bell, Gallaudet emphasized his desire to remain a gentleman. As to the specifics of what was said, Gallaudet did some backpedaling. His original statement (or alleged statement) accused Bell of stating untruths that were untrue "to his knowledge;" the new statement had Bell making remarks from which known facts had been omitted. The implication here was that Bell might have inadvertently left out the fact that deaf students would not be attending the normal school. Gallaudet was still convinced that Bell was in error, but now he was willing to admit that the error was accidental, not an effort to call him a liar.

Not surprisingly, Bell rejected this concession from Gallaudet. The assertion that he had omitted "important facts" which were supposedly known to him still rankled. He wrote Gallaudet, asking him to be specific in describing these facts. He also wrote to his wife, saying,

I have a shrewd suspicion that the "important facts" alluded to will be found fully discussed in my argument before the House Committee—but think it best to get him to make his charge definite before replying.

If the "important facts" turn out to be the facts that he proposed to receive hearing persons and to teach both the Sign and Oral Methods—and I suspect they will—it is a most extraordinary thing that he should not remember my discussing the questions—and comparing the Eclectic Training School to a National Theological Seminary in which all religions should be taught, etc. Can it be that he fails to perceive the distinction between his plans . . . and the plan before Congress— which is limited [by the language used] to the training of the graduates of the College. We shall see.[7]

Bell wondered whether Gallaudet failed to perceive a distinction in plans. Yet he also failed to perceive Gallaudet's own feelings. By repudiating Gallaudet's oral promise, he had said, in effect, "You are not to be trusted." If Bell could have understood this as Gallaudet's main complaint, the situation might possibly have been resolved. A simple change in the wording of the plan before Congress to include Gallaudet's promise not to accept deaf students into the normal school was all that was needed. Instead, Bell relied on Gallaudet's statements to Congress, which, in Bell's opinion, refuted Gallaudet's earlier promise by showing it to be impossible to keep. To Gallaudet, Bell's statements were irrelevant. Bell might be right or wrong, but Gallaudet had made a promise, one that he intended to keep. Bell could not understand this separation of logic and honor; he wrote to Mabel that he thought

> Gallaudet has lost his head—and has become so mad as to have forgotten all I said about hearing teachers—and Sign and Oral Methods, etc.—although it was said in his very presence.
>
> The most charitable explanation is to suppose that he has forgotten.[8]

While Bell was accusing his opponent of madness, Gallaudet was entertaining equally bitter thoughts about Bell. He wrote in his diary on March 19, 1891,

> In the evenings I was glad to stay at home and go to bed early for I was mortally tired—physically and mentally also weary of the name Graham Bell. I regard this whole matter of his opposition . . . as intensely discreditable to him.[9]

On March 21, a meeting of the Literary Society, of which both Bell and Gallaudet were members, was held at Bell's home. Neither Gallaudet nor any of the other members from the college attended, "not caring," as Gallaudet wrote, "to accept his hospitality just now."[10] Gallaudet's absence was certainly as much a relief to Bell as it was to Gallaudet.

On March 23, Gallaudet responded to Bell's request to be specific as to the "important facts" that Bell had omitted. He listed the following facts:

1. That the establishment of a school for the "training of deaf teachers of the deaf" was *not* "the purpose" of our proposed Normal Department;

2. That the plans for this new department included the training of hearing and speaking persons to be teachers of the deaf;

3. That in this department it was proposed to give the oral method equal prominence with the manual;

4. That it was proposed as an essential feature of the new department to give instruction in articulation to the students of the College;

5. That all these plans would be carried out next fall, if the appropriation of $5,000 asked of Congress should be granted.

These "important facts" were clearly laid before you at your house by me on Monday, January 26th, the day before you addressed the House Sub-Committee on Appropriations.

And yet the very next day the whole strength of your argument before the House Committee was directed against what you repeatedly declared to be my "proposition," vis: "to train deaf persons to teach the deaf," declaring at the close of your speech that the $5,000 asked for is *for this "purpose"* [italics added].

Am I mistaken in an impression I have received, that you have conducted your recent controversy with me more in the spirit and attitude of a lawyer (which you are not) bent on winning his case, than as a philanthropist (as I like to regard you) striving to advance a worthy cause?[11]

This last question was an attempt to say, Let's stop quibbling over who said what, when, and instead look beyond them to our own motives and feelings. Gallaudet was honestly working for what he felt were the best interests of deaf children, as well as his own personal and professional objectives. Bell, in his reply, seemed initially to reach out to Gallaudet in this spirit. He too, however, felt that he was protecting the best interests of deaf children. His letter gradually slipped from the conciliatory to the divisive.

I have told everyone of your intention to receive hearing persons and teach both the signs and oral methods. Indeed all of the points specified by you in your letter of the 23rd instant, which you charged me with omitting, are, as a matter of fact, mentioned, either in that argument or in your reply.

I did not mean to convey the idea that your intentions were limited to [a wrongful] end. I did not doubt that you intended to do more than that; but I believed, and still believe, that you could not do it under the wording of your application. . . .

Now I need hardly state to an experienced man like yourself, that what you say to me in my private parlor does not bind the expenditure of congressional funds. And while I have not ignored or omitted any of the important facts you stated to me, I felt bound to confine my argument, as much as possible, to the actual proposition before Congress. . . .

After careful examination of all your sayings and writings that by any possible construction might be considered to be before Congress . . . I fail to find any definite proposition to do more than train the graduates of your college to teach the deaf.[12]

Because all of the undergraduate students at the college were deaf, Bell concluded that if any of them went on to the normal school it would necessarily mean that deaf teachers were being trained to teach deaf students. In his letter to Gallaudet, he dissected the resolution that Congress had considered and explained that he interpreted it to mean that deaf students might enroll. The passage he quoted read as follows:

The amount submitted for current expenses is larger by $5,000 than the appropriation made for the current year. The object of this increase is to enable the directors to enlarge the facilities in the institution for normal instruction . . . As no normal school for the training of teachers of the deaf exists in this country, while several are sustained in Europe, it has been thought extremely desirable that the advantages for normal instruction existing in this institution to a limited degree should be increased.[13]

Bell also told Gallaudet

that, whether my construction be right or wrong, I have a perfect right to express my opinion without being charged with willful misrepresentation or falsehood. I have a perfect right to lay the matter before others and ask them whether they agree with me or not. That is all I have done, and I am sure that no fair-minded man will say that, because your judgment differs from mine, you are, therefore, justified in treating me with personal discourtesy.

You have impugned my motives . . . and you have publicly discredited me before the young men and women of your college, whose interests I have at heart.

Now I do not wish to write to you in any unkind spirit. I do not even write to demand the withdrawal of your remarks, for I care very little what people may say against my good name so long as the charges are unmerited and unjust. But I do care, that one who was my friend should entertain ungenerous thoughts concerning me, and, therefore, I have written you this letter in order to disabuse your mind.[14]

Bell must be given credit for breaking the impasse, or at least for providing a crack in the door. In the last paragraph quoted he stated that he was not demanding that Gallaudet withdraw his remarks. This represented a shift in the negotiations, one that allowed Gallaudet room to compromise. Bell's shift was not a concession or an admission that he had somehow seen the light and was bending to Gallaudet's wishes. Rather, Bell recognized that Gallaudet's feelings were hurt and would remain so despite his well-organized defense. Bell merely asserted that he too had feelings, as well as the right to express them, regardless of Gallaudet's opinion of their validity.

Gallaudet was quick to take advantage of this opening. He replied within twenty-four hours, suggesting that the two sit down together and "present each to the other his own 'point of view.' "[15] The Literary Society was to meet the next day at the college, and Gallaudet hoped that Bell and his wife might attend the meeting so that he and Bell could arrange for a private meeting later in the week. Bell turned this offer down. He wrote to Gallaudet that he was not averse to a meeting, but he refused to be seen on Gallaudet's home territory because it would "convey a false impression to our friends who would be there."[16] The false impression, of course, would be that Bell and Gallaudet had laid aside their differences. In addition, Bell's being seen at the college would be interpreted as a victory for Gallaudet—an impression Bell took pains to avoid.

The next day, April 2, Gallaudet repeated his invitation and offered to meet with Bell at the former's office. Bell replied, through his secretary, that he was busy on the suggested date. In addition Bell wanted it known that if and when the two men did meet, he was not willing to "enter into any verbal discussion concerning the matter in question principally because some misunderstandings between you (and me) have been charged to just such verbal discussions."[17]

Bell clarified his position in a letter to Gallaudet later that day.

> It is impossible for me to meet you in the friendly and cordial spirit we both desire until I have received your assurance that you are satisfied . . . that you no longer doubt either the purity and honesty of my motives or the desire and intention I had to represent your views truly and fairly.
>
> Once I have this assurance from you, I shall be most happy to meet you and trust that any remaining misunderstandings may be removed by friendly discussion.[18]

Bell was still not satisfied with Gallaudet's reply to his letter of March 30, in which he sought to "disabuse [Gallaudet's] mind" regarding his motives. For his part, Gallaudet had not replied to Bell that the letter had indeed disabused his mind; he merely wrote that he reciprocated Bell's sentiments. Bell wanted more.

> I appeal to you as a gentleman to say whether it is possible for me to talk over matters in a friendly spirit with one who hesitates to acknowledge me as an honorable man . . . .
>
> You pleaded your term examinations as an excuse for delay, but how long would it take you to write that, *if you really believed it in your heart?*
>
> There, sir, is the obstacle that prevents my further advances, *and its removal lies with you* . . . . I feel indignant that you should treat me as you do, and I am quite at a loss to understand the doubt and distrust that your acts imply. [italics added][19]

It was a confused and frustrated Gallaudet who, correspondence in hand, went to see President Welling of Columbian University. Gallaudet had sought his advice before, and Welling knew the specifics of the case. He advised Gallaudet to accept Bell's assurances that he had not intentionally misrepresented his views, and Gallaudet took his advice. He wrote Bell,

> I am sorry you did not give me the pleasure of seeing you, for had you done so, my first words would have given you the assurance you desired; viz, that yours of the 30th had satisfied me that you had not intentionally misrepresented my views in the recent discussions.[20]

Bell's reply, less than a day later, was one not of victory, but of relief.

> Your note of the 3rd instant just received has lifted a load of sorrow from my heart . . . . I feel now that I can set to work upon my Address for the Patent Centennial, with nothing to distract my mind, and you also can go on, undisturbed, with the work of the College. This will be good for both of us, and give time for many angry feelings to subside. Then we will write to one another again and endeavor to make clear whatever may be now obscure.
>
> If we approach each other in a spirit of perfect trust—if we assume as the necessary basis of friendly discussion the fact that, of course, neither of us are capable of dishonorable acts—then surely we shall be able to render complete satisfaction each to the other.[21]

On April 11, 1891—five weeks after the troublesome article appeared in the *Companion*—Bell and Gallaudet finally met face-to-face. They discussed their differences and agreed to disagree on the matter of methods. Gallaudet later wrote in his diary, "One good was gained— we can meet hereafter on a friendly basis . . . . The hatchet is buried, but I know where it is."[22]

This hatchet reference has been quoted by present-day historians as proof that Gallaudet never intended to coexist peacefully with Bell. Indeed, subsequent events resulted in a renewed and more bitter rivalry between the two. It is unlikely, however, that it was Gallaudet's intention to lie in waiting for the opportunity to take a figurative hatchet to Bell. Gallaudet was a cautious, even skeptical man, who was willing to let bygones be bygones; nonetheless he remained vigilantly on guard against his old nemesis.

Bell's attitude toward Gallaudet was no less skeptical; in fact it appears that Bell's efforts against Gallaudet only intensified after their public reconciliation. In a letter to a colleague in April 1892, Bell outlined his proposed plan of action.

The public agitation for an Oral Department at the National College should be continued. There is no harm in letting President Gallaudet have this idea that a fight is imminent in Congress, as the dread of a conflict that may injure the College and lead to a still further curtailment of his appropriations may operate as an element in inducing him to do better justice to oral work.

Our program I think should be 1st, public agitation concerning the relation of the National College to the Oral Schools of the Country— public agitation now . . . 2nd, Private discussion to elaborate a practicable scheme to establish a separate school for the higher education of the Deaf by the Oral method.[23]

While Bell's desire to advance his cause was praiseworthy, his method was less than honorable. Clearly, Bell's feelings toward Gallaudet, as well as his commitment to his cause, were no less intense and no more or less honorable than the feelings and commitment espoused by Gallaudet.

The Unification Battle

As the nineteenth century entered its last decade, many educators of deaf students were undecided as to how they stood on the communication methods issue. At this point, a good chance for reconciliation between the opposing sides still existed. Oralists and combinists might hold fast to their methods, but they could still work together on other issues, coexisting as colleagues working for the general welfare.

Gallaudet was a leading advocate in the movement to unify educators of deaf students into one common organization. He hoped that uniting the two groups into one association would benefit the entire field. One of the major obstacles was the innate animosity between the two professional organizations for teachers. The establishment of the American Association to Promote the Teaching of Speech to the Deaf (AAPTSD) in 1890 had created a rival organization to the Convention of American

Instructors of the Deaf (CAID). While there were people who joined both groups, oralists generally identified with the AAPTSD and combinists with the CAID. Bell, the impetus behind AAPTSD, had been receptive to the merger idea.

In 1892 the executive committee of CAID voted to adopt a merger plan. Coincidentally, the AAPTSD met at the same time as the CAID; on the day of the CAID merger vote, Bell announced that Philip Gillett, principal of the Illinois School for the Deaf, would be the new AAPTSD president. Gillett was a friend of both Bell's and Gallaudet's, and he had worked hard to reconcile Bell and Gallaudet after the normal school incident. Gallaudet interpreted Gillett's appointment as a signal that a merger between AAPTSD and CAID was imminent. By the end of the year, both Gillett and Bell had expressed support for *union* (as it was then called), though Bell admitted skepticism over the place of oralism in a unified organization.

It came as somewhat of a surprise, then, when Gillett wrote Gallaudet with the news that the AAPTSD had decided to postpone consideration of a merger. To Gallaudet this smacked of a power grab by Bell and represented a "bootlicking surrender by Dr. Gillett of his independence to Bell."[24] This situation stood throughout 1894 with no movement on either side. Gardiner Greene Hubbard did submit his own plan for union, but Gallaudet rejected it as worse than nothing because it called for an organization consisting of three groups—one more than currently existed.

By the summer of 1895 prospects for union looked dim. Gallaudet made an important decision to break off negotiations with Bell and take his cause directly to the people in the field. His forum was the CAID convention in Flint, Michigan. He was determined to show that his motives were good and that Bell, for personal reasons, had been responsible for blocking union. "It seems a great undertaking to 'do up' Professor Bell," wrote Gallaudet, "but I think it must be done. The material is abundant—and needs only to be used."[25]

On the opening day of the convention, Bell went on record as supporting union. He used as evidence the fact that his own group, the AAPTSD, had submitted a plan for union, and that this plan had been rejected. Gallaudet followed with an address that shook the entire field; he delivered a public and direct denunciation of A. G. Bell and his role in opposing the combined method.

Gallaudet started his speech with a description of the battle to establish the normal school at Gallaudet College, painting Bell as the villain for opposing it. Next, he blamed Bell for the current state of affairs (i.e., the existence of rival groups within the field). He even went so far as to ridicule Bell's association. Speaking through an interpreter and

using a slow Southern drawl he strung out the name . . . and (the interpreter) put the drawl into the manual alphabet by starting at one end of the long platform and walking slowly to the other, spelling laboriously, "T-h-e A-m-e-r-i-c-a-n A-s-s-o-c-i-a-t-i-o-n t-o P-r-o-m-o-t-e t-h-e T-e-a-c-h-i-n-g o-f S-p-e-e-c-h t-o T-h-e D-e-a-f." Everyone was smiling by the time the spelling was finished.[26]

It is unlikely that "everyone was smiling" at Gallaudet's speech. Bell had many supporters in the audience that day, one of whom characterized the speech as a "stigmatization of Bell as an unprofessional, narrowminded, despotic propagandist and intriguer for pure oralism."[27] Friends of Gallaudet saw it as simply a statement of facts. In Gallaudet's view, he had let the information speak for itself.

Bell, who was not present to hear Gallaudet, addressed the convention with a speech of his own. He spoke quietly and briefly, simply stating that Gallaudet had misinterpreted his motives. He expressed sorrow that the two groups could not work together in a more cooperative spirit, and he left it at that. His speech was viewed by oralists as the perfect response. One oral leader, Sarah Fuller, wrote,

He spoke as if inspired. I can only recall fragmentary portions, but the impression of the entire address was most delightful. Not a word of retaliation, not a thought of anything but entire truth . . . the speech was a model for the highest type of a Christian gentleman.

He lifted the entire audience into a broader, better, clearer atmosphere, and unconsciously, to himself, revealed what seems to me to be the secret of his great power over men—his intense desire to be true in everything he says and does.[28]

Gallaudet, on the other hand, characterized Bell's speech as lame and impotent. He attributed its brevity and lack of specificity to Bell's inability to dispute the facts.

In a dramatic moment during the last session of the convention,

> Dr. Mathieson, of the Ontario school, rose, and walking up to the
> front of the platform lifted his hands, [saying] "Let us have peace."
> Then turning to the crowded hall he asked those present to join him
> in a request to Dr. Bell and Dr. Gallaudet to shake hands and forget
> their differences. For a long tense moment neither man moved, but
> at last each stepped forward simultaneously, and the tips of their
> fingers met in a frigid handshake.[29]

One can imagine the two men, glaring at each other like two boys
on the school playground, neither wishing to make the first move of
reconciliation toward the other. Their handshake had the same significance as most forced truces. It was three and a half years before they
saw each other again, and then it was to join forces to push for a more
accurate and sensitive method of counting deaf people for census pur-
poses. By that time, oralists and combinists had gone their separate ways,
and any hopes for union had been dashed.

Bell's reaction to the entire incident was remarkably good humored.
In a letter to his wife, he wrote,

> Had a lively time at Flint—Gallaudet having made a most outrageous
> personal attack upon me and my work for the deaf. I was in good
> company though—the Oralists also—all-all of them were bad wicked
> people! And the A.A.P.T.S.D.—good gracious—such an infernal so-
> ciety evidently never existed before!—with its propaganda of "pure
> oralism."
>
> The address was simply "bosh"—to excite the passions of the deaf.
> Convention was largely packed with adult deaf-mutes . . . enough to
> swamp the votes of all the Supts. and Principals present.
>
> I am seriously troubled about Gallaudet—fancy he is not quite sane
> upon the subject of Bell and A.A.P.T.S.D. Don't think that any man
> in full possession of his senses would have written that address. I really
> do believe that he is suffering from mono-mania. At least that is the
> most charitable way to look at the matter. There has been insanity in
> his family—I understand.[30]

Mabel Bell was much less sympathetic than her husband. As long
as the dispute had been over educational methods, she had served as the

voice of reason. Now that Gallaudet had directly attacked her husband, her reason gave way to a less charitable personality. In a letter to her husband she described a reception at the National Geographic Society during which she encountered Gallaudet.

> I was sitting talking [to friends] and looking straight ahead when Dr. Gallaudet walked slowly past looking me full and steadily in the eyes, just as a dead man might and almost as white. His face never changed, his eyes never left mine until the slow walk had carried him past me and I, well, I went on laughing and talking and it is as I meant it should be and as it is right that it should be.[31]

In the same letter, Mabel Bell acknowledged that she and Gallaudet were at one time good friends. While admitting it was hard for her to feel poorly toward him, she felt that the effort was necessary. Her husband did not approve of her actions; he directed her to treat Gallaudet with respect.

> I don't approve of your carrying your resentment so far at all. I am very seriously of the opinion that he is only partly responsible for his actions—and that the future will reveal the fact of insanity taking the form of mono-mania against myself.[32]

Shortly after the Flint convention, Mabel Bell wrote Gallaudet a note in which she expressed her desire to sever all social ties between the two families. Gallaudet replied that he accepted, with reluctance, the severing of relations and reminded her that his Flint speech was not meant as a personal attack on her husband. Regardless of his intentions, the speech was interpreted personally, not only by the Bell family but by all oral educators.

If, through his speech, Gallaudet was attempting to take the cause of union directly to the people, he failed. Surely he must have foreseen the effect it would have. A more likely explanation is that Gallaudet knew that union had no chance. Rather than continue to spar with Bell, he thought it wiser to put distance between the two of them and the two schools of thought. A strong and forceful speech in the friendly environment of a CAID convention might have ended hopes of union, but it also would have solidified Gallaudet's position within the community of combined educators. If this was his objective, it was successful.

The CAID, before adjourning its convention, elected Gallaudet as its president, a position he held for 22 years until his death in 1917.

The Flint speech and its fallout created a schism in the field of deafness that exists to this day. Interestingly, there are those who welcomed such a schism. In a biography of Bell, Bruce likened the situation to "a pole standing on end ... the two forces pulling in opposite directions [oralist and combinist] are like guy wires, together being essential to the structure's stability. Such a balance of tensions is quite in the pragmatic tradition of American politics and society."[33]

While such tension may be an American tradition, it does little to improve the education of deaf children. Moores wrote that the oral/combined split after the Flint convention "precipitated an educational dark age."[34] The effect of the communications debate upon children has been considerable. Knowing this, and seeing how Bell and Gallaudet might have improved the situation, one cannot help but feel disappointed in these two leaders.

One might well ask why Bell and Gallaudet allowed the situation to deteriorate as it did. Both men were acting in what they perceived as the best interests of the children. Bell thought sign language was an obstacle to communication with the hearing world, and he fought it in the name of deaf children. Gallaudet, no less than Bell, believed in the rightness of his cause; he felt that oralism would deprive deaf children of the ability to freely communicate. In addition, factors other than children's interests were involved. A study of the Bell-Gallaudet relationship suggests that ambition and overgrown ego played a part as well. A true understanding of the situation requires a thorough analysis of both men and the communication philosophy that each espoused. Despite their great accomplishments and exalted status within the scientific and educational fields, both were, after all, only human. Seen in this light their actions and reactions may be easier to understand—if not easier to accept.

Sophia Fowler Gallaudet, 1865   Eliza Grace Symonds Bell, ca. 1880

Family Ties

THERE are no heroes or villains in this saga, even though most people in the field would disagree. Professionals have long taken sides based on their communication preference. One of the objectives of the present work is to show that neither Bell nor Gallaudet can easily be labeled; the actual situation was far too complex to be considered simply a fight between right and wrong. In order to understand Bell's and Gallaudet's strong stand for their respective positions, it is important to examine the backgrounds from which they came.

Much has been written regarding the influence of families on the formation of attitudes, beliefs, and values. There are obvious links between Bell's and Gallaudet's family backgrounds and their approaches to communicating with deaf students. The nature of these links differs, depending on the gender of the ancestor. The men in their lives exerted one type of influence, while the women had an entirely different effect.

All previous explanations of Bell's and Gallaudet's attitudes have centered solely on their fathers. This limited and one-dimensional analysis tells only a part, albeit an important one, of the story. In Bell's case, his grandfather also played a large and influential role. Bell's grandfather and father were elocutionists, public speakers, and speech therapists. Bell's father developed a theory of articulation and vocal expression that became known as Visible Speech. With two generations of elocutionists preceding him, it seems only natural that Bell himself should have come to value speech communication. Gallaudet's father was the father of education of deaf children in the United States. He based his pioneering efforts on the use of sign language; he signed fluently, and he forcefully advocated this method in numerous speeches and papers. It is hardly surprising that Edward chose to carry on his father's work and uphold his communication philosophy.

As compelling as these connections are, they tell only part of the story. They certainly explain why Bell was drawn to oralism and Gallaudet to sign language. They do not, however, explain the intensity of feelings that led each man not only to espouse a philosophy but to act as its champion. Further, each man's inability to compromise was hardly the result of his father's profession. As noted, other analyses of the communication issue have gone no further than to examine the fathers and their sons. While a deeper look provides no clearcut answers it does raise some important possibilities.

Bell's Grandfather and Father

A. G. Bell's father, Alexander Melville Bell, was not just an elocutionist and speech therapist. He was a highly intelligent, charismatic, and passionate crusader in his quest to lead the world to higher levels of civilization through the proper use of speech and language. A family friend described this passion after a visit to the Bell home as follows:

> I happened to be at his house on the memorable night when, busy in his den, there flashed upon him the idea [of Visible Speech]. . . . He took me into his den to tell me about it, and all that evening I could detect signs in his eye and voice of the exultation he was trying to suppress. At times it looked as if, like Archimedes, he might give vent to his emotions and shout "Eureka."[1]

With such a father, it is likely that Bell's enthusiasm and commitment came naturally. However, as a boy he was a poor student. While he was interested in his surroundings and constantly experimenting, he lacked the seriousness and sense of purpose that characterized his later life. It is unlikely that he ever would have found success in either the scientific or educational worlds if it had not been for his paternal grandfather, Alexander Bell. This Bell started off as a cobbler, became interested in the theater, and eventually translated his love of speech into a career as an elocutionist. When A. G. Bell was fifteen years old, he went to live in London with his grandfather for a year. This experience changed his life. As he later described it—

> This period of my life seems to me ... as the turning point of my whole career. It made me ashamed of my educational status—which was by no means high, and stirred up in me the ambition to remedy my educational limitations by my own exertions.[2]

These "exertions" began at the age of fifteen and ended only with his death sixty years later. Bell's need to know so consumed him that he became a student of everything. He would stay up until four o'clock in the morning as a matter of habit, reading, thinking, and writing what he called his "Thoughts." A short selection of titles from these "Thoughts" shows the breadth of Bell's interests over a lifetime of curiosity and invention.

1. Rockets
2. Warming and Cooling by Radiation
3. Sheep Breeding
4. Suggested Remedy for Certain Kinds of Neurologic Pains
5. Ventilation and Heating of Houses
6. Weather Forecasts
7. What to Do with the House of Lords
8. When Does a Profit Become Usury?
9. Why Does a Cream Pitcher Have a Protecting Lip?

Bell's transformation into a lifelong student was the work of his grandfather. The year in London with him made Bell, in his words, "ashamed of ignorance. I threw aside fairy tales and novels and took to study."[3] It was never enough for Bell to know something of a subject; he had to be an expert in anything he did. Once back with his father, he resumed his study of elocution with new-found zeal. This enthusiasm, when added to his exceptional intelligence and even more impressive imagination, resulted in the making of a genius. Who else could have taught a dog to talk?

> When I was a young man ... I began to wonder whether the mouth of ... a dog would be capable of producing articulate sounds. We had a very intelligent skye terrier, and upon this creature I began to make experiments ... Taking his muzzle in my hand, I caused his lips to close and open a number of times in succession while he growled. In this way he gave utterance to the syllables "ma, ma, ma." After a little practice I was able to make him say, with perfect distinctness, the word "mamma," pronounced in the English way with the accent on the second syllable.
>
> I then placed my thumb under his lower jaw, between the bones, and pushing up a number of times in succession, I caused the dog to pronounce the syllables "ga, ga, ga."
>
> By careful manipulation of the muzzle, we obtained a sound that passed for "ah," and, by finishing off the "ah" sound with a final "oo," we obtained a diphthongal vowel that passed for "ow" (as in the word "now").
>
> The culmination of this linguistic education was reached when the dog was able to say in an intelligible manner the complete sentence, "How are you grandmamma?"[4]

This story reveals more than Bell's expertise in handling four-legged animals. It shows his imagination, creativity, and tenaciousness. He would not give up on something until he had seen it through, and he would not abandon a belief, regardless of the evidence, if he felt it was worthwhile or correct. These traits, acquired in childhood, shaped Bell's entire life. They permitted him to continue fiddling with coils of wire in what others saw as a vain attempt to transmit the human voice over great distances. They also permitted him to emerge as the educational and political leader of oral communication and to defend that philosophy against all critics. Bell's grandfather imbued in him the curiosity and thoroughness of the scholar. His father served as an example of a deeply committed experimenter and as a promoter of his own causes. These factors, when added to his oral tradition, make a good beginning toward understanding the complete Alexander Graham Bell.

Gallaudet's Father

Edward Miner Gallaudet's father was no less an example and inspiration to his son. There were two areas in particular in which his father influenced him. The first of these was religion. Thomas Hopkins Gallaudet, a deeply spiritual man, was an ordained Congregationalist minister. His children were raised in an atmosphere that stressed religiosity and responsibility. The other area of influence was in career choice. The elder Gallaudet taught deaf children, and his son followed in his footsteps. Likewise, T. H. Gallaudet was an advocate of signing, and so too was his son. As noted earlier, however, Edward Gallaudet had initially balked at joining the profession. He wanted money, and teaching deaf children was hardly the road to riches or even moderate wealth. In addition, Gallaudet wanted prestige. While his father had attained a respected reputation for his work with deaf children, Edward did not feel that he could duplicate that attainment.

There was, however, one thing that Edward Gallaudet wanted more than either fame or money, and that was to please his father. It was very important to him that his father approve of and, if possible, take pride in him. When T. H. Gallaudet died in 1851, it came as quite a blow to his youngest son. Edward had not, at age fourteen, decided what he would do with his life, nor had he received the approval from his father that he desired. His father's death did not allow him to abandon the need to please; if anything, it intensified it. In April of 1856, five years after his father's death, Gallaudet had a mystical experience that illustrates this compulsion to please his late father. As he described it,

> I was sitting this evening in my sister's room . . . playing on the piano when my attention was attracted by the peculiar appearance of my father's portrait that hangs directly over the piano. Some irresistible influence invited my eyes upon it and it looked upon me and smiled; and as those clear loving eyes that had so often gazed upon me while they shone in life seemed now to speak with life-like earnestness, I looked back upon the past and reviewed the events of my short existence.

I commenced at childhood and as I thought of the guileless happy years I thru passed, the portrait seemed to be thinking just as I was, for it looked pleased at the remembrance of those years when innocence beamed brightly on my brow.

I passed onto boyhood and the picture assumed an anxious look for anxiety and watchfulness had been the accompaniments of my boyish days. Thru one after another of the actions of my life came before my memorie (sic) and as I looked at the picture, it seemed to change countenance in unison with the changes in my mind—and when I reached the present time I looked intently to see whether I was to be approved or disapproved and I saw a mingled expression of sadness and warning.

Alas I am not what I once hoped I was. I am not what I would be, and I am not what, with God's strength, I hope to be again.[5]

Teaching deaf children was one career option, but Gallaudet was still drawn to the world of business. The experience at the piano had an effect on him, however, and less than a year later he had taken a position as a teacher at the American Asylum in Hartford. One year later he accepted the superintendency in Washington that occupied him for the rest of his working life. What seems like an obvious progression to some was in reality a bumpy road with many detours. In truth, Thomas Hopkins Gallaudet exerted his biggest influence over his son after his death because of Edward's great need to please his father. Edward Gallaudet never again wrote of the incident at the piano, nor is there any record of his returning to the house at the end of his life to see whether his father's portrait showed pleasure or disappointment.

Bell's Mother and Wife

While Bell's and Gallaudet's male relatives influenced their choice of occupation, their female relatives greatly affected their individual approaches to their work. Bell's oralism and Gallaudet's manualism were not totally the products of their fathers' examples. Crucial to their communication philosophies were their expectations for deaf people. The primary women in their lives were themselves deaf, and it is through them that each man undoubtedly developed his communication philosophy. Thus it is important that these women be examined to see what sort of examples they set and to see how they influenced expectations that led to communication approaches.

There were two deaf women in Bell's life, his mother and his wife. Eliza Bell, his mother, had become hearing impaired after acquiring speech and language, and she never lost her skill in either area. The extent of her hearing loss, while substantial, was not complete. She could play the piano and could conduct conversations with the aid of an ear trumpet. Throughout Bell's childhood and up until he was in his twenties, postlingual deafness was the only deafness he ever encountered. This must have affected his attitude about educating deaf students. It certainly influenced his stance on speechreading. Eliza Bell could never read lips, a situation she lamented but accepted as inevitable. Bell's father, though a strong proponent of speech training, thought that similar training in speechreading was a waste of time. Alec, observing his own mother's failure to read lips, agreed with his father until he had the chance to leave home and observe deaf people who were skilled in the art.

Another important point regarding Bell's mother was her lack of interest in associating with other deaf people. Her world was made up entirely of hearing people; in fact, she never formed close relationships with anyone deaf, with the exception of her son's wife, Mabel. Her ability to succeed and be happy in the hearing world made a deep impression on her son, who came to feel that the use of sign language would prevent the type of integration he so closely observed.

While Eliza Bell influenced her son's expectations, another deaf woman far surpassed her in the effect she had on his thinking. From the time of their courtship in 1873 until Bell's death in 1922, Mabel Hubbard Bell was the most important person in his life. The association of Bell and his assistant, Thomas Watson, has been portrayed by Hollywood, but the Alec-Mabel relationship was truly the stuff of the silver screen. Such was her loving and positive effect on him that he was rarely able to refuse her a request. For example, when Bell did not wish to travel to Philadelphia to exhibit his telephone at the Centennial Exhibition, she was able to convince him to change his mind. He agreed to go for a buggy ride with her, not knowing that she had secretly bought a train ticket to Philadelphia and had hidden his packed suitcase in the buggy. Upon arrival at the station, when he still refused to board the train, she "burst into tears and said, 'I think you might do this just to please me. If you won't do a little thing like this now, I won't marry you.'"[6] Bell boarded the train, went to Philadelphia, and exhibited the telephone. Had he not made the trip, others might have established claim to the original design of the invention.

Mabel Hubbard Bell did more than act as her husband's travel agent. Her ability to succeed and excel as a deaf person in a hearing world did much to form Bell's communication philosophy and his expectations for what deaf students could accomplish. Mabel Bell was a strong and self-assured woman whose excellent speech and speechreading skills allowed her to mix comfortably with hearing people, regardless of the situation. She took her children to Europe, where she communicated easily with foreign speakers. Her fluency in German, when added to her amazing ability to read lips, allowed her to act as interpreter for other members of her family whose hearing was normal.

It is important to note that Mabel Bell's skills in oral communications were not then, and are not now, the norm. It had been generally thought that Mabel Hubbard lost her hearing and all her speech and language skills as a very young child. If this were true, it would have made her abilities even more amazing and would have constituted an excellent recommendation for the oral method. However, a collection of private correspondence found in the Bell Papers at the Library of Congress tells a different story. These letters show that her initial loss of speech and hearing was not as serious as was commonly assumed. They prove that Mabel Hubbard lost her hearing at age five, later than even she herself had thought. Further, they show that she never lost her ability to speak. This news came as a mild shock to Mabel Bell.

> I have always understood that I completely lost all knowledge of speech, and it had to be laboriously restored to me. But these letters, written at the time, do not bear this out. They rather indicate that I never quite lost the power of speech, and my mother's task was rather to help me retain what I had and from that to teach me more language.[7]

The Bells did not learn the truth about Mabel's hearing loss until 1919, when the letters referred to were found. For more than forty years Bell had fought for the oral method, using as his example the success of his own wife. But the example was bogus. He was convinced that children born deaf, and therefore unable to naturally acquire speech and language, could nonetheless attain good oral skills. His conviction may well have been weakened had he known the true nature and extent of his wife's hearing loss.

Even considering the real extent of her disability, Mabel Hubbard Bell was an amazing success story. Her speech skills were excellent (no thanks to her husband, who refused to take the role of speech teacher with his own wife). Her speechreading ability was such that she could converse easily in two-party conversations, only rarely asking for repetition. Her most amazing skill was in language, where she far surpassed the typical deaf person, regardless of age at onset or degree of loss. Consider her own reminiscence describing her early childhood—

> I did not care to romp and play out of doors, all I wanted was to curl up in some quiet corner and read—all day long if allowed. My father's library was well stocked and I had almost free range. When eleven years old I delighted in reading such books as Jane Porter's *Scottish Chiefs*, and before I was thirteen I had read through, with intense interest, *Motley's Rise of the Dutch Republic*, most of Prescott's histories, several large volumes of the Civil War, books of travel, as well as all the stories and novels I could get hold of."[8]

The average thirteen-year-old deaf child has neither the ability nor the interest to read *The Rise of the Dutch Republic*, nor for that matter does the average hearing child of that age. This reminiscence shows three things: first, that Mabel Hubbard's interests and abilities were far superior to those of deaf children her age; second, that her life as a child was scholastic, revolving mainly around books; and third, that the result of her voracious reading habit was an ability to use language at a level far beyond the normal deaf adult. This third point is all-important; Mabel Bell's writing shows evidence of exceptional English language development when compared with the typical deaf adult's ability. Teachers of deaf students would agree that such phrases as "I did not care to romp and play," "curl up in a quiet corner," and "delighted in reading," reveal unusual facility with the English language. While only teachers might appreciate the significance of those phrases, anyone can recognize Mabel Bell's skill in the following piece. Titled "World of Silence," it is a personal description of how deafness felt to her and how she understood the concept of sound. Despite its length, it is repeated in its entirety because it so clearly makes the case for Mabel Bell's exceptional ability and because it reads so beautifully.

WORLD OF SILENCE

It is the universal habit to think of those who cannot hear as dwelling in a "world of silence." Even those who come most frequently in contact with the deaf as teachers or relatives, even the deaf themselves, refer to them as living in silence. The very idea of deafness—is it not supposed to mean inability to hear sounds—what therefore is so correct as to say that to be deaf is to be immersed in silence or soundlessness.

Yet I who of all persons am thus steeped in soundlessness—through whose golden gates of hearing no sound of the living world may pass, am conscious of no habitual lack of sound. Perhaps it is correct to describe the blind as living in darkness. On the contrary I am intensely, acutely conscious of those rare moments when my world is indeed silent—voices may not come to me through the broken nerves of sound—the melody of birds unseen makes no ripples on the sound waves of my world, but there is no silence in the birds' rapid flight across my field of vision. Whenever I see a leaf stir there is the feeling, the sensation at least of sound. It is a wonderful conception surely, yet a true one, that seen motion implies the sensation of sound.

I know what the world of silence is. It is the silence of a hot sabbath morning in the country—Summer, when no breath of air stirs the smallest twig—when the cattle lie still—the waters of the lake show no ripple—not the faintest breath of wind fans the face—no clouds float by—no life, animal or mammal, stirs. Then there is silence complete and profound—a silence that is stillness—what those who hear call a hush, when all nature seems waiting in breathless silence. That is silence to me also. And then comes a faint ripple across the glass-like waters—a twig moves, a cow flicks his tail—and the silence is broken to me as well as to him whose ear rather than eye noticed the change. The soundlessness still exists materially, but the difference between the material of the outside world and the power of one's imagination is so slight that the effect is the same to the brain reached through the eye nerve as to that through the ear nerve.

And so it is with everything. The hoarse roar of the city streets, it comes to me also—a very faint reflection of the wild tumult of sound as it is to you of the ear nerves perhaps, but answering its purpose of breaking up the silence. The various noises of a house shaking in the storm or under heavy footsteps make noises more or less distinct. The flash of a woman's garment past a door—the breath of wind moving the curtain—the flicker of the sunshine—the passage of a fly on the ceiling—in short movement of any kind whether perceived through the eye nerves or coming as sensations perceived through the body, all felt through sensation nerves or perhaps merely through association, represent sound to me—and represent it so acutely that it seems to be mine is a world of constant sound—of sound that is constantly rising and striking or varying in intensity—but it is so rarely silent that when it is silent I become instantly aware of it and when this silence is long contained am oppressed by it.[9]

Mabel Hubbard Bell's skill was clearly exceptional, and the importance of that fact to the present study cannot be minimized. Alexander Graham Bell looked to his wife as an example of what typical deaf people could accomplish using the oral method. He never acknowledged that his wife was atypical or exceptional. Ironically, the pivotal person in his conceptualization of a communication philosophy may have inadvertently misled him and, undoubtedly, reinforced his resolve to stick unbendingly to oralism. One may hypothesize that, had Bell married a "typical" deaf woman, he might not have been such a staunch oralist. However, Bell could not abide the ordinary in anything or anyone, and it would have been impossible for him to marry an ordinary woman, be she hearing or deaf.

Gallaudet's Mother and Wives

Sophia Fowler Gallaudet had as profound an influence on her son as Eliza Bell had on her son. Sophia Gallaudet remained the primary female relationship in Edward's life. She provided Edward's model of what a happy and successful deaf adult should be. She also epitomized the typical adult in the nineteenth century.

Sophia Gallaudet did not receive any formal educational instruction until she was nineteen years of age. In her nineteenth year she enrolled at the American Asylum in Hartford. Up until then she had "passed through childhood to young womanhood, with scarcely a glimpse at the ample page of knowledge. She received no mental instruction, save through the disconnected natural signs of her friends, which could hardly treat of more than the objects of vision."[10] While Eliza Bell had difficulties speechreading, Sophia Fowler was barely able to read a single sentence. She remained a student at Thomas Gallaudet's Hartford school for only four years, during which time "her acquirements were confined to the common English branches."[11] The end to her formal education came when she married Thomas Gallaudet, and it never continued.

One wonders at Thomas Gallaudet's choice of a wife, especially since Sophia was entirely unable to join him in intellectual discourse or to play much of a part in social gatherings. The answer may lie in his zeal to save and uplift deaf people. A close friend wrote of the marriage,

> As it confirmed his opinions, privately and publicly expressed, concerning that class, so it redoubled his ardor to elevate them. It [the marriage] was ... the strongest sanction he could give to his belief that members of that class needed only the light of education to enable them to share in the enjoyments of civilization, and participate in the cheer of Christian hopes.[12]

One need not feel sorry for Sophia Gallaudet. Her world was every bit as happy and fulfilling as her husband's. While Thomas Gallaudet was busy making his reputation in the world of letters, Sophia Gallaudet was busy raising a family. This was a noble pursuit in an age of intense domesticity. Her success in managing the household expenses and in raising eight children stood her in good stead within the community. Her husband seemed satisfied as well, though his close friend Amos Draper later wrote, "as the years went on ... he found himself sometimes compelled to notice the disparity of their intellectual acquirements."[13]

Sophia Gallaudet undoubtedly helped shape her son Edward's conception of the successful deaf adult. Her oral skills were not good, but she was able to communicate all she wished by using signs. Surely, Gallaudet looked beyond his mother's third-grade reading level and lack of speech when formulating his expectations of deaf students' potential. He realized that his mother's condition was due, in large part, to the fact that she had received no education until her nineteenth year. He eventually was among the first to speak in favor of lowering the starting school age for deaf students, so impressed was he with the need for early intervention.

The important point is that Gallaudet had been exposed to a deaf person who, by using manual methods, felt happy and fulfilled as an individual. Not only did he grow up with this example, but he brought his mother with him to serve as matron when he took the superintendency of the Columbia Institution in Washington, D.C. Sophia Gallaudet's example eventually affected the expectations of an entire faculty and student body.

Unlike Bell, and even his own father, Edward Gallaudet married twice, both times to women with normal hearing. From all indications, his first marriage was built less on love than on his desire to end bachelorhood and gain greater respectability in the community. Only a month after his wife's death, he wrote, "Now I can live!"[14] Gallaudet's second marriage, to Susan Denison in 1868, was somewhat more successful. In his diary, he wrote that "no giddy youth of one and twenty was ever more hopelessly, perhaps even foolishly in love than was I, a staid experienced man of the world of thirty-one winters."[15]

Despite this profession of love, the Gallaudets had their problems. Susan Gallaudet had recurring headaches and other illnesses that often caused her to be separated from her husband. To compound matters, she seemed to be comfortable only when around members of her own family. The couple lived apart for long periods of time because of Mrs. Gallaudet's illnesses and because of Gallaudet's responsibilities and obligations as president of Gallaudet College. In addition to this, it seems that Edward and Susan Gallaudet had few mutual interests. Gallaudet's diaries show that when he had something important to discuss or needed a shoulder for support, he went to a close male companion, of which there were several during his lifetime.

Gallaudet also revealed in his diary a secret in his life, one that was so troubling that he couldn't even discuss it with his closest associates. In fact, the pages of his diary on which he disclosed this secret have since been ripped out, perhaps by Gallaudet himself. This unmentionable secret, added to his two marriages and his close male relationships, lead to speculation that Gallaudet may have had homosexual relationships or inclinations. If true, it would certainly have been something he would have wished to hide, given nineteenth century attitudes toward sexual differences. Homosexuality might even have been a factor in Gallaudet's ready acceptance of deaf people and their sign language because he understood what it meant to be different and he respected those differences. Though this supposition is only speculative, it may explain, in part, Gallaudet's long-standing belief that deaf people were not inferior, they merely couldn't hear.

Comparisons

The differences between Mabel Bell and Sophia Gallaudet were major factors in the communications debate. A key difference in the nineteenth century oral and combined philosophies was the expected outcome of each approach. The oralists advocated integration as the primary desired outcome. While not eschewing language skills and other academic attainments, they saw these more as means to an end, that end being assimilation. The combinists, in turn, did not reject integration as a desirable outcome. To them, however, it was not crucial; their emphasis was on the intellectual and social development of the individual. If a person was never able or willing to integrate into the hearing world, but instead found contentment as a well-educated and employed person within the smaller deaf community, the combinists' goal would be achieved.

It is worth noting that Mabel Bell not only integrated easily into the hearing world, she actually despised the deaf world. She often refused to accompany her husband to meetings or gatherings of deaf adults and she studiously avoided making their acquaintance. She was obviously proud of her place in the hearing world and, perhaps, did not wish to be reminded that were it not for her unusual intelligence and oral skills, she might herself be living in the deaf subculture. Gallaudet's mother, unlike Bell's, was of average intelligence and had minimal oral skills. She required the use of sign language in order to learn, to grow as an individual, and to find a place in the world. When one considers these models, and adds to them the emphases of the other Bells and Gallaudets already discussed, the making of two divergent philosophies begins to take focus.

Alexander Graham Bell, ca. 1918

Personal Philosophies

ALEXANDER Graham Bell and Edward Miner Gallaudet both came from families that exerted vital, influential roles in each man's development. As important as these family influences were, however, they do not wholly account for the differing philosophies each man espoused. Bell and Gallaudet had their own unique ways of making sense of the world. Bell painted with large, broad brushstrokes that put society's needs before those of individuals, while Gallaudet used a finer technique that emphasized individuals and their needs. What they each developed was a philosophy of life and of each individual's place in society. Bell and Gallaudet not only translated these differing philosophies into opposing methods of teaching deaf children, they applied these same beliefs to the world beyond education and extended them from the deaf to the hearing population.

Bell's Social Perspective

Millions of people know Alexander Graham Bell invented the telephone. A far smaller number know of his work in educating deaf children. Still fewer people know that Bell was a major figure in the intellectual movement known as Social Darwinism, particularly that branch known as *eugenics*. Social Darwinists applied Charles Darwin's theory of the survival of the fittest to the social structure of the day. Darwin saw different species of plants and animals in a constant struggle to survive; success came through the adjustment and compromise known as evolution. Social Darwinists applied this analysis of nature to human society. They saw competition as a social law (as well as a law of nature) and survival as the reward of the fittest.

Eugenicists applied Darwin's theory to the task of developing a fitter race through selective breeding and a program to keep America free of inferior peoples. In the vast evolutionary panorama of the Social Darwinists, white Anglo Saxons were the vanguard of evolution. The darker races and the inferior and debased stock (including the handicapped) lagged far behind. Eugenicists were not concerned as much with individuals as they were with society, and they hoped to improve society through selective immigration and controlled marriages and childbearing, primitive forms of what today is known as genetic engineering.[1]

Many eugenicists carried this idea to its extreme. Having decided what the *ideal* man and woman should be, they advocated such policies as banning all future immigration; prohibiting interracial marriage; and sterilizing retarded, blind, and deaf people. These and other policies were aimed at improving the race; if certain individuals suffered in the process, so be it. Bell, while sharing the goal of race improvement, did not join the extremist fringe of the movement. He called the extremists cacogenicists because they concentrated on society's negative aspects instead of seeking to encourage positive attributes. Bell's general philosophy was that,

> given a large normal class and two small classes, the desirable and undesirable, the problem is, how to increase the proportion of desirable children born from the normal population. . . . If, then, we wish to improve the race the aim should be to increase the potency of the desirable class to produce desirable children; and this can be accomplished by promoting the marriages of the desirables with one another.

The moment we have a body of desirable persons whose parents were also desirable, improvement of the race begins through the marriage of such persons with the normal population.[2]

Bell saw the encouragement of good marriages as a positive approach to race improvement, and he contrasted it with the negative approach espoused by some others. He did not generally support enactment of laws prohibiting marriages with or between *undesirables*. After carefully studying the problem, he had concluded that undesirables were not the products of undesirable parents, but most often were the offspring of normal parents.

It is to be regretted that the efforts of eugenicists have been mainly directed to the diminution of the undesirable class . . . we shall always have the undesirable with us, because they are sprung mainly from the normal class; and it is more practicable to improve the undesirable strains than to eradicate them.[3]

While it is comforting to hear Bell rejected the eradication of "undesirable strains," one cannot help but take note of his rational justification. The following quote causes one to wonder whether Bell would have felt differently if eradication had been seen as an effective tool for improving the race:

We have all sorts of strange and fantastic schemes for improving the race by instituting legislative interference with the marriages of the undesirable; but I have seen clearly that this would not produce the desired improvement, for even were we to go to the extreme length of killing off the undesirables altogether so that they could not propagate their kind, this would not lead to an increase in the quantity or quality of the desirable, it would simply prevent deterioration. It would diminish the production of the undesirable without increasing the production of the desirable.[4]

These words are chilling, particularly to twentieth-century readers. It can be argued that Bell saw the scientific argument as being more effective than the humanistic in weakening support for extreme measures. Nowhere, however, not even in his personal papers, does he reveal concern for the individual undesirables who would be eradicated, sterilized, or prevented from marrying if the extremists had their way.

Still, Bell did not openly support such measures. Instead, he called for the breeding of clearly superior people. He envisioned the development of a thoroughbred strain of humans who would then intermarry to improve the entire race.

> In any large aggregate of individuals the vast majority will be of the average type of the race. Some few will be markedly superior and some few inferior.... Superior individuals on the whole have a larger proportion of superior offspring than the average of the race. Of course in cases where both parents were superior this prepotency is increased. It would be still further increased if all the four grandparents were superior, and if three or four generations of ancestors were all individually superior, a thoroughbred would be produced.

> In the case of men and women who are thoroughbred ... it is obvious that their descendants, spreading out among the population and marrying into average or inferior families, would prove prepotent over their partners in marriage in affecting the offspring, thus leading to an increase in the proportion of superior offspring produced from the average or inferior with whom they have mated.... There would thus be a general advance in the possession of desirable qualities all along the line from the lowest to the highest. Is not this what we mean by improvement of the species?[5]

Bell believed that improvement of the race would result from rational matchmaking, not from government regulation. But who would determine the actual plan and select the individuals to implement it? The problem, wrote Bell,

> is one of great difficulty and perplexity, for its solution depends upon the possibility of controlling the production of offspring from human beings. By no process of compulsion can this be done. The controlling power ... resides exclusively with the individuals most immediately concerned ... so that our processes should be persuasive rather than mandatory.[6]

The question of persuasion vs. compulsion arose constantly in Bell's work with eugenics. There was one area in which Bell did advocate government intervention, and that was over the question of who should be allowed to enter the country. Many Social Darwinists took a dim view of immigration. What was the sense of trying to improve the race from within, they asked, when undesirables from outside were pouring into the country, diluting their efforts? Bell's voice joined the chorus of those who looked disparagingly at immigrants. His wife, in commenting on his views, wrote, "Alec used to give me information of the most miscellaneous kind, and we often got into political discussion; Alec holding much to my disgust that America was the refuge for the ruffians of the whole world."[7]

Some Social Darwinists advocated closing the *Golden Doors* to the United States entirely. Others, like Bell, advocated a selective approach.

> The grand spectacle is presented to our eyes of a new people being gradually evolved in the United States by the mingling together of the different races of the world in varying proportions. It is of the greatest consequence to us that the final result should be the evolution of a higher and nobler type of man in America, and not deterioration of the nation.[8]

In Bell's view, the wave of immigration hitting America's shores in the late nineteenth and early twentieth centuries was potentially good for the country if the right groups were admitted. Government control was needed, however, to weed out the undesirables. Bell felt that

> the process of evolution should be carefully studied and then controlled by suitable immigration laws tending to eliminate undesirable ethnical elements, and to stimulate the admission of elements assimilated readily by our population and that tend to raise the standard of manhood here.[9]

A few years later, Bell became alarmed at the types of people being admitted to the United States. He was especially concerned because, as he saw it, "it is undoubtedly the fact that in America the children of foreign-born parents are increasing at a much greater rate than the children of native-born parents—and the position is sufficiently grave for serious consideration."[10] Bell saw this "fact" as an issue of self-preservation. "The only hope for a truly American race," he wrote, "lies in the restriction of immigration."[11] He was never specific, however, as to who should and should not be allowed into the country.

In 1915 an effort was made in Congress to require all potential immigrants to take an English literacy test. Failure on such a test would mean a trip back to the country of origin for the unlucky or illiterate immigrant. Proponents of the test contended that illiterates put too great a strain on society. Opponents countered by noting that many immigrants were escaping some sort of persecution and that if denied entry to the United States, they might face imprisonment or worse back home. This human rights argument did not move Bell. He took what he thought to be a more rational, scientific approach.

> Literacy is a product of education and environment rather than of heredity.... There can be no doubt, I think, that the literacy test may deprive the United States of much good new blood which would be of benefit to the people.

> On the other hand . . . an ignorant voter may be a source of danger . . . it should not be forgotten that the proportion of unfit is probably greater among the illiterate than the literate—so that the test may be of benefit as well as harm.[12]

Though Bell saw both good and bad in the literacy requirement, he recommended that the immigration bill, including the literacy requirement, be passed. He had weighed the pros and cons as they affected society and ignored the consequences for the individuals involved.

In addition to literacy, Bell was concerned about immigrants' national origin. He suggested that the United States would do well to copy Canada's immigration policy. At that time, Canada accepted all immigrants for a three-year probationary period. The Canadian government reserved the right to expel any immigrant during that period. "There are few undesirable citizens," wrote Bell, "who can live three years in a country without showing themselves to be either good citizens or bad ones—and if bad they are gotten rid of."[13] What most impressed Bell about Canada's system was

> the positiveness of which Canada knows the kind of people she needs and wants, and her determination to have only that kind. The immigration Commissioner has in his own mind drawn a line through the center of Europe, separating the Northern people from the Southern. He takes Finns, Germans, English, Russians, and Hollanders— all who are farmers and farm-working people, who will make the land productive and who do not desire to mass in the cities.[14]

Immigrants to the south of the immigration commissioner's line were generally thought of as less educated, less cultured, and less American-like than their northern neighbors. In agreeing with the Canadian immigration policy, Bell made clear his belief that admitting southern Europeans into the country would pollute the otherwise clean and pure elements that the United States needed to maintain its superior stock. He apparently ignored the fact that both he and his father had been immigrants and that though they were northern Europeans, they had settled in cities, not on farms.

It seems obvious that Bell saw the question of immigration as part of the larger issue of race improvement. His frame of reference did not include individuals, but rather the society they comprised. This fact is significant, as it will help to explain Bell's philosophy of education for deaf children.

It is one thing to maintain beliefs and another thing to put those beliefs into practice. The ways in which Bell implemented his philosophy supply further proof that, given a choice between individual freedom and societal well-being, he compromised the former for the latter. He was comfortable in publicly advocating government restriction of immigration, but he was not nearly so candid on the issue of marriage. He knew that any effort to regulate marriage would meet with strong opposition. Instead of compulsion, he advocated persuasion.

> We may as well recognize, first as last, that we have no power to compel improvement. . . . All desire that their offspring may be of the best; and no one wishes to have degenerate or defective children. The attitude of the public mind is therefore favorable to voluntary compliance with plans which appeal to the intelligence of the community as reasonable and right, and favorable to the formation of a public opinion which will compel compliance.[15]

While this statement indicates that no force should be used to interfere with anyone wishing to marry, a careful reading of the last phrase—"formation of a public opinion which will compel compliance"—gives one pause. Bell seemed to be hinting that community pressure might be directed against those who, in the opinion of the community, should not marry. At times his remarks seemed benign, simply a statement that intelligent people, armed with the facts, would act rationally and accordingly: "If it should be clearly shown that certain classes of marriages are hurtful to the offspring and others beneficial, the mere dissemination of that knowledge would by itself tend to promote desirable and prevent undesirable unions of the sexes."[16]

Yet, one cannot help feeling that Bell favored some form of compulsion short of actual legal mandates. "The ever-present altruistic sentiment of the community," he wrote, "is not opposed to prevention, but on the other hand will cooperate freely with intelligence to bring this about."[17]

Bell himself had a number of plans designed to encourage intelligent breeding. For example, he regarded long-livedness as both desirable and inheritable, and he hoped that a disposition toward this trait would influence the choosing of mates. To this end he wrote,

> It is therefore important to collect information concerning the long-lived ancestry of very young persons, even school children, so that the information collected may be absorbed by the parents and friends, and the young people themselves, long before any entanglements of affection have appeared.
>
> Where cases are discovered in which an abnormal proportion of the ancestors lived to extreme old age, the parents would not object to the publication of these names.[18]

Bell was certainly not trying to harm those who did not have a tendency toward long life. Rather, he saw the publication of the list as an aid to those who, like himself, valued long-livedness and wished to pass it on to their children. That it would indeed hurt average or short-lived families did not occur to Bell, or at least did not concern him.

He put forward a similar though potentially more dangerous plan that judged not just life span but good health in all its aspects.

> Suppose that a law should be passed compelling all males when they arrive at the age of 21 years to submit themselves to a physical examination in the interests of the War Department.... In a case where the person is certified to be physically fit for military service the document really constitutes a certificate of good health and vigor and freedom from defects that would disqualify him for military service.[19]

Such a plan is similar to those currently in existence in a number of countries. However, as Bell developed his scheme, he found a new and somewhat forbidding application for the certificate of good health.

> The enlightened public opinion would consider young men who have successfully passed their physical examination as more eligible in marriage than others. . . . It is safe to say that most men who have been declared physically fit would not conceal the fact and their friends would know it. An enlightened public opinion would leave them to be proud of the fact and most of those who would conceal the result of their examination would belong to the class of not physically fit.

> The known possession of such a certificate might often give a young man an advantage over his rivals who were not known to possess certificates and the more I think of it the more I believe . . . that the granting of certificates . . . would constitute a most important means in promoting the marriages of the physically fit young men.[20]

Bell apparently gave no thought to the rights of those who might be injured through their inability to pass a government fitness test. Indeed, he saw the certificates as a means of weeding out such undesirables. He believed that,

> fathers and mothers of marriageable daughters, to say nothing of the daughters themselves, would be anxious to know whether a proposed suitor has . . . a certificate of physical fitness; and many stern fathers doubtless would demand the production of such a certificate before giving their consent to marriage with their daughters.[21]

Bell's last step would send today's civil libertarians running to the courthouse.

> As a matter of public policy, government appointments . . . should be given as much as possible to such persons . . . so that salaries derived from the appropriations of public money should be as much as possible expended upon healthy persons who are contributing to the production of the healthy and strong in the community.

> It would certainly be of benefit to the whole people to have government appointments so made as to encourage the production of offspring from the healthy and strong.[22]

According to Bell, then, not only were those in poor health to be shunned in marriage; they were also to be denied government jobs! While Bell's plan might ultimately have benefited his notion of the ideal society, its negative impact on individual liberties would seem to far outweigh its possible advantages.

Bell was not totally insensitive to the rights of individuals. He simply placed more importance on group needs. He likened society to a beehive and individuals to bees living in hexagonal cells—

> The approximation of individuals in social life demands the restriction of individual liberty into the hexagonal form. . . . The individual whose regard for others is greater than his regard for his own rights has his cell crushed in, and distorted by outside pressure. If he is unmindful of the rights of others he expands to the detriment of neighboring cells, and interferes with the due coordination of the whole community, producing not simply a distorted cell, but a distortion of the fabric of the community itself—a distorted honeycomb instead of a distorted cell.[23]

Individual liberty was therefore important, but only so long as it was acceptable to the community. If the community felt it necessary, it could abridge that liberty. Such intervention, Bell thought, might be necessary to ensure against the spread of weak or undesirable elements within society.

> Among the inalienable rights recognized by the Declaration of Independence are "life, liberty, and the pursuit of happiness." The community has no right to interfere with the liberty of the individual and his pursuit of happiness in marriage unless the interests of the community are demonstrably endangered. . . . The production of undesirable children is, of course, an injury to the community, and there may perhaps be cases where legal checks may be justified. . . . Legal prohibition of marriage should only be resorted to in cases where there could be no manner of doubt that the community would suffer as the result of the marriage.[24]

This kind of intervention is commonplace in the late twentieth century. Laws prohibiting the marriage of first cousins, for example, are designed to prevent the birth of handicapped children. These laws are generally accepted by all segments of society. Yet in the century of Auschwitz the drift of Bell's argument sounds ominous. The problem arises when society attempts to broaden its definition of what constitutes *undesirables*. It would seem important that those responsible for establishing the definition think not only of society's needs but of individuals' rights as well. This, Bell admitted, was difficult for him to do. In a letter to his wife he wrote, "You are always so thoughtful of others—whereas I somehow or other appear to be more interested in things than people—in people wholesale, rather than in persons individual."[25]

Years later, Bell's son, Gilbert Grosvenor, described his father's self-assessment as a "very accurate description of Dr. Alexander Graham Bell; his interest was in mankind 'wholesale'."[26]

The theme of society vs. the individual is particularly relevant when analyzing Bell's involvement with deaf people. Critics of oralism have contended that it is less an educational tool than it is a social policy. Its aim, they contend, is not to prepare the individual to learn and achieve up to his or her potential, but rather to allow the individual to become a participating member of the larger society. It is society, with its own needs and expectations, that is important, and entry into it is the goal of oral education. Bell would no doubt agree—up to a point. Good oral skills are crucial to successful integration, and integration is a basic part of the oral philosophy that Bell espoused. However, did Bell maintain that integration into society was important because society demanded it or because the individual would be happiest as a member of that society? This is an important question, and its answer has implications not only for nineteenth century education but for current practices as well.

Bell's work in eugenics exemplified his concern with societal rather than with individual human needs. When his life's work is viewed in this light, it becomes clear that his interest in deafness was eugenic as much as it was educational. This is not to say that he lacked empathy for the individual deaf children whose lives he so profoundly affected. However, a strong case can be made that Bell thought more about the effect of deafness on society than on the lives of deaf persons themselves. Even his staunchest supporter and ally, his wife, complained to him that "your deaf-mute business is hardly human to you. You are very tender and gentle to the deaf children, but their interest to you lies in their being deaf, not in their humanity, at least only in part."[27]

In 1883, Bell presented a paper to the National Academy of Sciences entitled *Memoir Upon the Formation of a Deaf Variety of the Human*

Race.[28] In it, he asserted that the deaf subculture in the United States was growing at an alarming rate and that steps should be considered to halt this state of affairs. While he could not alter the inheritability of deafness, he could address the issue of intermarriage among deaf people. He suggested two types of measures to reduce intermarriage—preventive and repressive. The preventive measures he advocated included an end to the segregation of deaf students in special schools, an end to the employment of deaf teachers for deaf students, and an end to the use of sign language. These three practices "produce an environment that is unfavorable to the cultivation of articulation and speechreading,"[29] and without those skills, Bell maintained, how could deaf people expect to attract hearing mates?

Bell's repressive measures included calling on friends of deaf people "to prevent undesirable intermarriages,"[30] even though he doubted that friends would be willing to interfere in this way. He suggested a law banning all intermarriage among deaf couples, but immediately rejected it as impractical. It would, he wrote, only foster immorality, though he did not specify whether such immorality would result from covert marriage or covert coupling. Another law he suggested would have banned intermarriage only in cases where one or both individuals were congenitally deaf. This too he rejected as unworkable since establishing etiology would be impossible in many cases. The most workable law, Bell wrote, forbade the intermarriage of deaf persons from families with at least one other deaf member. It is important to note that Bell did not advocate immediate passage of any of these laws. He called first for more data collection and more study, and then he concluded that "due consideration of all the objections renders it doubtful whether legislative interference with the marriage of the deaf would be advisable."[31] Even though legislative restrictions might be a good idea, Bell decided the ensuing furor would cause more problems than the restrictions themselves would solve.

Bell's *Memoir* deeply offended members of the deaf community, who rightly regarded it as an attempt to legislate them out of existence. His statement that such legislation was not advisable did not soothe them, and the majority of deaf adults thereafter viewed Bell with disdain and fear. For his part, Bell maintained that he did not advocate legislative interference. He accused deaf people of misinterpreting his writing due to their poor reading ability.

The *Memoir* was addressed to the highest scientific body in the land, and the languge used is therefore probably beyond the comprehension of a large proportion of the deaf. This perhaps may be the reason why the deaf, as a class, have relied upon second-hand information concerning its contents.[32]

Perhaps the deaf community did misinterpret Bell. Or perhaps they were reading between the lines, seeing not a moral aversion to restrictive laws but instead a practical view that such laws, while needed, were politically difficult.

Legal prohibitions aside, Bell did speak out forcefully against intermarriage of deaf adults. He tried to convince educational leaders to join him, but was generally frustrated. "We cannot but note with alarm," he wrote, "that many of the most prominent teachers of the deaf in America advocate the intermarriage of deaf-mutes."[33] Bell was no more successful with people close to him. One of Bell's first students, George Sanders, became a close and life-long friend. Imagine, then, how Bell felt after learning that Sanders planned to marry a congenitally deaf woman. He expressed his frustration in a letter to his wife—

I am afraid the attachment has become too strong for prudence to have sway. They will surely marry—but what then? Will lovers ever consider the good of those that will come after them? Deafness has come down through four generations to Miss Swett, yet prudence will not prevent her from marrying one who was born deaf—and George chooses danger to his offspring—for her love. Yet I can understand it too.[34]

So strongly did Bell believe in the negative effects of intermarriage that he requested and received permission to speak on the subject to the faculty and students at the National Deaf-Mute College. He began by refuting the belief that he supported legal restrictions on marriage.

It is a very difficult thing for me to speak to you upon that subject, because I know that an idea has gone forth, and is very generally believed in by the deaf of this country, that I want to prevent you from marrying as you choose, and that I have tried to pass a law to interfere with your marriages. But, my friends, it is not true. I have never done such a thing, nor do I intend to; and before I speak upon

this subject I want you distinctly to understand that I have no intention
of interfering with your liberty of marriage. You can marry whom
you choose, and I hope you will be happy.[35]

He followed this with a statement that may well have destroyed his
credibility with his deaf audience.

It is the duty of every good man and every good woman to remember
that children follow marriage, and I am sure that there is no one
among the deaf who desires to have his affliction handed down to his
children.[36]

What Bell failed to comprehend was that, to many deaf people,
deafness was not an affliction, but rather a simple fact of life. Bell saw
deaf people as different, as less well-equipped than those who could
hear. It never occurred to him that there were some deaf people who
were satisfied with their condition, who considered themselves normal,
and who saw nothing wrong with having deaf children. To be told by
a hearing person that they were "afflicted," and that none of them would
wish to pass on this affliction, was surely an insult. One may argue
whether deafness is an undesirable affliction, but has anyone the right
to make that decision for others? This is what Bell did, and doubtless
his view had the backing of society in general. He should have known
that it might not have the backing of deaf people.

While clearly giving priority to society's needs, Bell honestly believed
that he was working in the best interests of the deaf community. In his
speech at the college, he also said,

You have to live in a world of hearing and speaking people, and
everything that will help you to mingle with hearing and speaking
people will promote your welfare and happiness. A hearing partner
will wed you to the hearing world and be of inestimable value to you
in all the relations of life. Not only will your own success in life be
thereby increased, but the welfare of your children will be materially
promoted.[37]

Here Bell was obviously speaking to his perceptions of what deaf
people themselves needed. It was his opinion that many deaf people
would marry hearing partners, if it were not for their fear that such

marriages would be unsuccessful. He encouraged them to try, using some dubious mathematical evidence as sweetener.

> Do not let anyone place in your minds the idea that such a marriage cannot be a happy one. . . . The chances are infinitely in your favor that out of the millions of hearing persons in this country you may be able to find one with whom you may be happy than that you should find one among the smaller numbers of the deaf.[38]

The larger pool of potential hearing partners was actually irrelevant, since the very fact that they were not deaf put them all at a distinct disadvantage when compared to the smaller number of potential deaf mates. The important point was Bell's insistence that a good marriage with a hearing partner was greatly to be desired, not only for the sake of the children (and society), but for the happiness of the deaf partner as well.

One more eugenic application requires note. Like all Social Darwinists, Bell was convinced that the fittest would ultimately survive. He applied his belief to educational programs as well as to different races. He was convinced that in a struggle for ascendancy between oral and combined methods, the oral method (the fittest) would prevail. During the debate over establishment of the Normal School in Washington, D.C., Bell stated,

> All I want is fair play among the methods and equal treatment of all. I would say to the Government "Hands off—let them fight it out among themselves." I have full confidence that the struggle will end in the survival of the fittest if only the Government can be induced to let them alone.[39]

After examining the state of affairs in 1894, Bell was convinced that evolution had already made its mark. Ever since the Milan Convention of 1880 had voted overwhelmingly to support oral education, the number of oral schools in Europe and the United States had been on the rise. Bell was moved to comment that

> natural selection, operating on the continent of Europe for more than a century, has brought about the survival of the pure oral method and the almost total extinction of the French system of signs. The verdict of time is therefore conclusive as to the superiority of the oral over the sign method of instructing the deaf.[40]

If Bell were alive today he would realize that the verdict is still very much in doubt. While oralism was in ascendancy in the late nineteenth and early twentieth centuries, it is on the decline in the late twentieth century. As late as 1915, approximately sixty-five percent of classes for deaf students were oral and thirty-five percent were combined. But by 1976, nearly sixty-five percent of the classes were combined, while only thirty-five percent were oral.[41] Indeed, to a Social Darwinist this might indicate that the combined and not the oral system is more likely to survive.

Bell, the eugenicist, thought it best for the race that all people be able to hear and, short of that, that all people at least be able to understand speech and communicate orally. Bell, the educator, espoused the oral method and stressed integration while at the same time addressing the academic needs of deaf children. That Bell became a staunch oralist should come as no surprise considering his family background and his vision of an improved society.

Gallaudet's Individualist Perspective

In writing of Gallaudet's philosophy of education and, indeed, of life, the paucity of reliable background material must be noted. Unlike Bell, whose interests and writings spanned dozens of subjects, Gallaudet confined himself almost entirely to the subject of education of deaf students. With the exception of an unremarkable book on international law and some minor jottings, everything he wrote pertained to deafness. It is unfair, however, to compare him to Bell in this regard. Bell, besides possessing a brilliant mind and an insatiable curiosity, had another reason for leaving an extensive bibliography. The invention of the telephone was a bittersweet experience for him; it led to years of hearings and litigation over patent rights. Bell himself was partly to blame for this because he had not taken care to document all of his work. This lack of written evidence opened the door for others to establish claims on the invention. Bell eventually prevailed, but only after much mental and emotional duress. He never forgot this experience, and for the rest of his life took care to document his affairs carefully—thus, the rich lode of primary sources. The dearth of material by Gallaudet must simply be accepted and borne in mind when analyzing his work.

Gallaudet did not share Bell's scientific and rational view of the world. Rather than view things as they affected society, he thought in terms of individuals and families. There are several possible explanations for this. First of all, Gallaudet did not equate deafness with deviance. He had grown up with a deaf mother who had capably raised a family, worked, and coped in a hearing world. Gallaudet also knew many deaf adults who led productive and fulfilled lives.

Another reason Gallaudet may have emphasized the importance of individuals was his strong belief in religious, moral, and social responsibility. Gallaudet's father was a Congregationalist minister, and Gallaudet himself had considered such a vocation. He believed it important that deaf children receive religious and moral instruction, and this belief played a large part in his support of sign language. He rejected the notion that an inability to hear and speak were the only, or even the most important, consequences of deafness.

> That there is a deaf-mutism more deplorable than that which is merely physical will be well understood by all who have met with un-educated deaf-mutes of mature age. Our compassion for these is not more called forth by the consideration that their ears are closed . . . and their tongues useless . . . than by the reflection that their minds are dwarfed, their sensibilities undeveloped, their social natures warped and soured, their moral perceptions nebulous, and their religious feelings unawakened.[42]

Gallaudet looked beyond the outward signs of deafness and focused instead on the effect they had on the whole child. He carried this focus over to education, where he claimed "the aim should be to secure the highest possible development to the greatest possible number, morally, mentally, and physically."[43] He did not believe that oralism ignored moral, mental, and physical development, but rather that it considered them secondary in importance to oral skills. He simply reversed the priorities.

Gallaudet believed that once the needs of the deaf child were accepted in the broad sense, the importance of speech was diminished. He went so far as to say that

> under the Manual Method, with oral teaching entirely omitted, the intellectual, moral, and religious training of the whole body of the deaf can be effected much more completely than under the Oral Method . . . the

lack of speech is an inconvenience, but by no means an insuperable barrier to success in business or the attainment of happiness.[44]

Bell, of course, could hardly agree that a lack of speech was an "inconvenience." To him it was crucial, and to those who disagreed he wrote,

> Do not let us be misled by the idea that intelligible but defective speech is of no use, and must necessarily be painful and disagreeable to all who hear it. Those who have seen the tears of joy shed by a mother over the first utterances of her deaf child will tell you a different tale. None but a parent can fully appreciate how sweet and pleasant may be the imperfect articulation of a deaf child.[45]

Gallaudet knew that parents desired speech. He did not, however, feel that such parental desires should hold sway. While Bell sided with parents in supporting speech, Gallaudet's argument was based on his perceptions of the needs of deaf children.

> A majority of parents are more delighted with even an imperfect development of speech in their deaf children than with their intellectual attainments. And yet we all know that the mere power of vocal utterance is of slight importance compared with an ability to read and write, a knowledge of figures, a comprehension of the ordinary facts of history, geography and natural science, not to speak of the higher flights of learning, the development of character and the cultivation of religion.[46]

Communication with God was just as important to Gallaudet as communication with peers. To him, "the object of deaf-mute education [was] . . . to break down, as far as circumstances will permit, the barriers raised by their physical infirmities in the way of their free intercourse with their race and its Maker."[47]

To that end, Gallaudet recommended that "moral training should be carefully attended and . . . religious instruction of an undenominational character should be afforded."[48] Not only should religion be a formal part of the curriculum, but the principal of the ideal school should be "a man . . . of earnest religious convictions, prepared to inspire and develop veneration for God and the highest moral aims."[49]

Bell did not share Gallaudet's religious zeal. "My religion is all of the practical kind," wrote Bell. "I hold no theories or beliefs whatever."[50]

Still, moral virtue was as important to him as it was to Gallaudet. They differed only on the place moral education should have in the classroom. Gallaudet, unlike Bell, saw it as affecting every part of the child's education. In addition, he felt that only through the use of signs could moral instruction be successful. In this he echoed the view of his father, who wrote,

> Let it never be forgotten that in order to exercise a successful moral influence over the child . . . his confidence in his guide and governor must be secured. In cultivating this confidence he must often be listened to patiently by the parent and teacher. . . . For all these purposes the child must have a language at command, common to him and the teacher, by which to make his thoughts and feelings known.[51]

The language referred to is, of course, sign language. How, Gallaudet reasoned, could a child receive moral instruction when all of his or her time was spent learning to communicate? In a combined program, such communication came easily, so moral and religious instruction need not await acquisition of improved oral skills.

Gallaudet clearly viewed the combined method as superior to other methods for meeting the spiritual needs of children. Not only did he reject oralism as a means of imparting spiritual values, he even went so far as to describe oralism itself as being immoral. In a paper written in 1900, he asked, "Is there anything in the process of the oral education of the deaf which has a tendency to impair the moral sense of those people who engage in it, either as teachers or pupils?"[52] He answered his own question by relating an experience with an oral deaf child who had come to a convention to demonstrate her skills. Gallaudet caught her signing and asked her if signs were allowed at her school. "Yes," she replied, "but Mr. _____ told us we must not make any signs here, and I forgot." Noticing her apparent ability to hear him, he then asked her if she indeed could hear. Again the reply, "Yes, but Mr. _____ told me I must not let it be known that I hear."[53] The incident angered Gallaudet.

> Are not these injunctions to conceal facts of a piece with what often occurs when the speech of deaf children is being exhibited and visitors are lead to conclude that those before them were born deaf, when in fact many of them, and these generally the most fluent speakers, either possessed some hearing, or had acquired speech before becoming deaf?

> Is it not common for oral teachers to assure their pupils that if they
> exert themselves to succeed with speech, they may avoid being rec-
> ognized as deaf persons, may appear "just like other people," in short,
> that they may "deceive others?"

> If in their sincere enthusiasm to impart the great boon of speech to as
> many deaf children as possible, some oral teachers plant seeds of un-
> truthfulness in the minds of their pupils, a very high, even a ruinous
> price is being paid for an accomplishment that is found in many cases
> to be of comparatively little practical value.[54]

The fact that combined programs were probably equally guilty of
deception by exhibiting their best students to visitors and policymakers
apparently did not occur to Gallaudet. His sense of right and wrong
was offended by the ruse, and he was particularly incensed that children
should be brought into the plot.

Honesty was important to Gallaudet, a man who believed fervently
in a life after death, a life available only to those who did good works
on earth. As his diary entry on his birthday in 1891 shows, he fully intended
to qualify.

> I am fifty-four today, and highly blessed in health, wealth, success in
> my work, with a family also in health, children of great promise, and
> a reasonable hope of immortal life when the short limit of my earthly
> existence shall be reached. Much to make me hopeful and cheerful, in
> spite of the fact that the years of *this* life slip so rapidly by.[55]

To Gallaudet, work with deaf people was a crusade. He was fighting
God's battle on earth, and in fact thought that he had the support of
God in the battle over communication methods. Shortly after winning
his fight to establish the normal school at the college, he wrote, "Bell
has made it hard for me, but Providence has helped."[56] With a group
of deaf adults at a convention, he prayed,

> He who guides the stars in their courses answers even the silent prayer
> of the voiceless, and with firm trust in Him we will labor without
> wearying, doing our part to hasten the advent of the time when every
> deaf child that can speak shall speak, when all shall have the best and
> the most education they are capable of receiving, when the most ef-
> fective methods shall be employed in every school, and when every
> heart shall be filled with His love.[57]

Gallaudet had faith that eventually God would ensure that "the most effective methods will be employed in every school." It isn't difficult to determine which of the methods God would choose. Though he never said so, Gallaudet clearly believed that God was an advocate of the combined method.

Gallaudet's emphasis on moral and religious values seems to support the notion that he held a humanistic view of life, in marked contrast to the scientific view held by Bell. This difference may provide a simple yet compelling explanation for the entire communication methods debate— oralists think of society's needs while combinists think of the children themselves. But such an explanation overlooks one important point: Concern for individuals is not necessarily a humanistic perspective.

Gallaudet's speeches, papers, letters, and diaries reveal great concern for deaf children, but always based on his own perceptions of their needs. High moral values were important, but whose values were they? Spiritual needs required attention, but who determined those needs? In neither case were the children consulted. It is likely that Gallaudet, as well as Bell, regarded deaf children as less able, less qualified, and less normal than their hearing brothers and sisters. His views on marriage support that likelihood. Surprisingly, Gallaudet agreed with Bell that a deaf person should, when the condition was hereditary, marry a hearing person.

> Were my advice sought by a young deaf-mute, heart-free, and un-
> trammelled by any engagement, I should say that if he or she could
> marry, on a basis of sincere affection, one possessed of hearing, such
> a union would be far more to be desired than one with a deaf partner.[58]

This jeopardizes the hypothesis that Gallaudet thought first of the individual. Would he not support the deaf person in marrying whomever he or she chose? Indeed, Gallaudet was so strongly against marriage between deaf people that he advocated celibacy for some deaf adults.

> I have several personal friends who have remained unmarried because
> of the existence in their families of certain mental or physical defects
> likely to descend to offspring; and as I honor them for their unsel-
> fishness, so would I rank high in my esteem a deaf person who lived
> single for a similar reason.[59]

By urging against intermarriage, Gallaudet allied himself with Bell. Still, this attitude does not forfeit his claim to speak in the best interests of deaf individuals. Gallaudet merely determined, rightly or wrongly, that the children who might be born of a mixed marriage would have a better chance in life than the children of a deaf union. In short, it was better to be hearing than to be deaf. Therefore, for the good of the children, deaf adults should increase their children's chances of being able to hear by marrying a hearing partner.

While Bell and Gallaudet did agree that a deaf adult should choose a hearing spouse, their justification and motives differed. Their agreement may nonetheless disappoint admirers of Gallaudet who would like to believe that he placed no stigma on deafness whatsoever. In his defense, it should be noted that Gallaudet was indeed a progressive educator when viewed in the context of the nineteenth century. In the days before John Dewey and Carl Rogers, education, particularly for handicapped children, was aimed at fulfilling the needs of society. Gallaudet's concern with individual children was unusual, despite his view that it was better to be hearing than to be deaf. Few people today, deaf or hearing, would argue with that view.

Bell and Gallaudet held two different attitudes toward deafness, which resulted in two different approaches to education. Bell saw any deviancy, including deafness, as bad for society, and he searched for ways to eliminate or reduce the number of deaf people. For those people born deaf, he believed that an oral education would enable them to integrate into society. There, they would be more likely to meet and marry hearing spouses, thus reducing the future deaf population. Gallaudet was concerned more with what was best for the individual deaf person. He maintained that if sign language would aid a person in developing his or her full potential, then it should be used.

Alexander Melville Bell, 1868

Alexander Graham Bell, 1876

Alec and Mabel Bell with their daughters
Elsie and Marian (Daisy), 1885

Alexander Melville Bell enjoying his pipe while his
granddaughter Elsie talks to her grandmother
(Eliza Bell) through a speaking tube, ca. 1885

Alexander Graham Bell and his wife,
Mabel Hubbard Bell, Nova Scotia, 1909

Alexander Graham Bell, 1910

Alexander Graham Bell (right) at a meeting in
Cold Spring Harbor, Long Island, 1915

Thomas Hopkins Gallaudet, ca. 1850   Edward Miner Gallaudet, 1859

Edward Miner Gallaudet and family on the porch of House One (Gallaudet College), ca. 1885
(l to r: Herbert, Marion, Susy, Kitty, Grace, E. M., Edson, Denison)

Above: The Kendall Green Tennis Club, ca. 1891
(E. M. Gallaudet holding tennis racket)

Left: Edward Miner Gallaudet, 1867

Right: Edward Miner Gallaudet, 1875

Below: An outing entitled "Pan Cakes for Dinner," 1899
(E. M. Gallaudet seated at right)

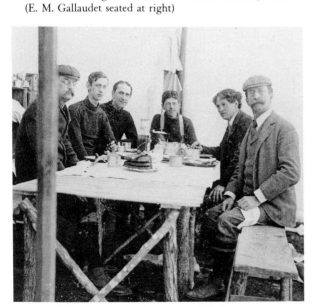

Alexander Graham Bell's school at 1234 16th Street, NW,
Washington, D. C. The school opened in 1884 for deaf and
hearing children. Bell's two daughters attended the school.

The Columbia Institution for the Deaf and Dumb, Washington, D. C.
(now Gallaudet University), 1878

The Boston School for the Deaf, June 21, 1871
(A. G. Bell at top right)

Students and faculty at the Columbia Institution for the Deaf and Dumb, 1867
(E. M. Gallaudet seated at middle)

Fourth Summer Meeting of the American Association for the Promotion of Teaching Speech to the Deaf, Chautauqua, New York, July 3–13, 1894 (E. M. Gallaudet seated in first row, 4th from right; A. G. Bell standing in back row, center)

Eighth Meeting of the Convention of American Instructors of the Deaf, Belleville, Ontario, Canada, July 15–20, 1874 (E. M. Gallaudet standing in 2nd row, 4th from left, A. G. Bell standing in 2nd row, behind woman in striped dress)

Above left: Helen Keller (left), Annie Sullivan, and Alexander Graham Bell communicating in tactile sign language, 1894

Above right: Glove used in the early 1870s to teach deaf children. A. G. Bell used a similar glove when teaching George Sanders.

Laying of the cornerstone of Kendall School dormitory (now Dawes House), 1895 (E. M. Gallaudet is standing at center, signing "house")

EIGHT

Edward Miner Gallaudet, 1916   Alexander Graham Bell, 1902

Legacies

IN many ways, the current situation within the field of education of deaf children can be traced to the efforts of Bell and Gallaudet. The Volta Bureau, the A. G. Bell Association for the Deaf, and the *Volta Review* are all results of Bell's work, and all are actively involved in carrying the banner of oralism. The Convention of American Instructors of the Deaf and the *American Annals of the Deaf* are present-day manifestations of Gallaudet's original efforts, and both support the use of sign language. Further, just as little has changed within schools for deaf children, little has changed in the debate over communication methods. Indeed, it would appear that the attitudes and expectations that motivated Bell and Gallaudet in the nineteenth century may be the very ones that continue to form the basis for disagreement today.

This chapter presents a brief survey of the expectations of teachers and parents. Parental feelings and attitudes are particularly important because parents are often the ultimate decisionmakers in the communications debate. In order to sketch this picture as accurately as possible, a representative sample of parents and professionals was interviewed to determine how individuals make their own personal choices between oralism and some system that includes sign language. From the responses, it is clear that today's debate centers on the very issues that were important in the nineteenth century (i.e., the question of what is normal and the dialectic between individual and societal rights and goals). All the responses quoted in this chapter were shared under conditions of confidentiality; therefore, no attributions are included.

Choosing Sides

Both Bell and Gallaudet were born into families that had a definite communication preference. Bell's family had a strong speech-orientation. His father and grandfather taught elocution, and his mother spoke well despite her deafness. Gallaudet's entire family used signs. His father had been the principal of a residential school where everyone signed, and his mother signed but did not have very intelligible speech.

Most parents and teachers don't come from such backgrounds; they make their choices for different reasons. Indeed, there is usually a surprising lack of thought and consideration given to the choice. At times, people do not even realize they are making an important decision. Prospective teachers frequently come to the field without an intelligently developed opinion about communication methods. Rather than choose a training program to fit a philosophy, many develop a philosophy that fits the norms of the training program. One teacher admitted,

> I really had no idea that a division existed within the field. I just knew that I wanted to teach the deaf. I checked a few college catalogs and applied to a program. It so happened that I ended up in a program that believed in the combined method. In fact, it wasn't until about three months into the program that I realized there was another point of view.

If a prospective teacher is exposed to a single deaf child, that child's communication style will likely determine what method the teacher adopts. This point was clearly illustrated by the teacher who reported that his parents owned a house, and at one time new neighbors moved in. They had a boy who had been ill at birth, and we watched him grow into a boy with no speech at all. He didn't talk, and made funny noises. He was diagnosed as being deaf and started out in an oral school. I viewed his classes, and was very impressed.

Not surprisingly, this respondent enrolled in a training program that prepared him to teach in a setting similar to the one he had observed— one that advocated a purely oral approach.

Once teachers are trained in a particular method they are likely to be steadfast supporters of that method. Repudiating one's roots requires a repudiation of teachers and colleagues, as well as an admission that one's original training and experience had been in error. Such an admission among educators of deaf children is rare, comparable to a priest's renunciation of his vows.

Parents present a somewhat different case, though serendipity still plays a role. As one father said, "As chance would have it, we got in contact with oral people first, and I think that was a factor." It seems likely, though, that parents make their choice based on their own expectations and one or two programs they actually see in operation. One mother who eventually chose oralism stated,

When you read about the combined method, God, it sounds so good! The kids on the one hand are supposed to talk, on the other hand they have this great tool for expressing themselves through signs—but when I observed programs, I realized that what the combined method says it will do for the child, and the way it's practiced, is a whole different game. In the programs I observed, kids relied upon signing exclusively. That's the one objection that I had, that I didn't see it working.

This parent was looking for speech and valued it over language. When she saw children signing without speech she rejected the program. Some parents make the opposite choice. After viewing an oral program one mother felt "depressed. All they did was work on speech. No history, social studies, or even math. Talking isn't that important to me." This parent placed more importance on intellectual attainment than on oral communication, so she placed her child in a combined program. While neither parent had knowledge of the Bell-Gallaudet debate, their choices were clearly made based on the same arguments.

One very important factor that affects parents' choice of methods is the testimony of experts. A mother remembered her pediatrician's recommendation that her child be enrolled in an oral program immediately so that he would learn to talk and to read lips. When she told this doctor that she was considering a program that used sign language, he informed her that if she chose it, he would refuse to treat the child. Though no formal surveys have been made, it is likely that the majority of medical doctors recommend oral programs over programs that include sign language. The *medical model* values a healthy and fit individual, one with the ability to speak and hear. It is a model in perfect harmony with Bell's. Gallaudet would also have accepted the model, but would have expanded it to include social and emotional well-being—factors frequently neglected by medical professionals.

Parents do not often have the strength and confidence to defy these experts and tend to accept their word as gospel. This blind acceptance often creates a one-sided picture. Note the following conversation:

Question: Why did you choose the Clarke School? [an oral school]

Answer: One of the four best in the country.

Question: What are the other three?

Answer: Central Institute for the Deaf [oral], Lexington [oral], and the third would be the John Tracy Clinic [oral]. I mean, these are the things people see when they come from around the world.

Clearly, this woman had not received a complete picture of what was available to her. The schools she listed may all be very good, but they are also all oral.

A tremendous amount of pressure is put upon parents to make the "right" decision for their child. Indeed, parents are often held accountable for their child's success in school, particularly in oral programs. Oralists frequently assert that every child should have the chance to be oral. In their view, parents who choose combined programs rob their children of any chance to speak, speechread, and integrate into hearing society. Another assertion claims that young deaf children who learn sign language cannot or will not afterwards learn to speak. Research has provided data that counters both of these assertions, but parents continue to feel the pressure.

The more closely involved the parents are in the communication choice, regardless of the final decision, the more bound they will feel to make it a success. The argument between oralists and combinists thus puts a great deal of pressure on parents, but it should be the educators themselves who feel the pressure to excel. A father expressed this pressure well by saying,

> It is very hard for a parent who is experiencing the traumatic shock of finding out that his child is deaf to make judgments, when he is exposed to this conflicting maze of opinions of so-called experts. Each side will defend its philosophy very strongly, and is going to bring out arguments that do make sense. If the experts cannot agree among themselves, what can the parent make out of this situation.?

While serendipity and experts' opinions affect the parents' choice of communication method, the experts themselves remain divided for the same reasons that divided Bell and Gallaudet. The goal for oralists is still a student who will be successful in the hearing world. Subject matter is important, but not if integration skills are sacrificed. Combinists are more likely to sacrifice speech for language; they emphasize language development at an early age. Once a child has passed the age of five, language learning is more difficult and often unsuccessful. An advocate of the combined method explained,

> I see it as easier for parents to give feedback on the kids' speech if communication is happening and they know, for example, that the kid is saying "milk" and isn't just doing some kind of unintelligible vo-calization. The mother or father is going to have the opportunity to say, "Oh, you want some milk, milk, milk, milk" repeating the sign and saying the word simultaneously.

The emphasis here is on early communication, something that is difficult when children and parents must rely on speech and speechread-ing. Oralists put less emphasis on early parent-child understanding than they do on the eventual goal of communicating with the outside, speaking world. This hope was voiced by an oral parent.

In my judgment, the oral approach is perhaps the more risky but more ambitious, in the sense that it would enable the child to establish better rapport with the outside world by being more oral, as opposed to relying upon more signs. We'd like to see if our son can do the best possible that his handicap will allow. If a child comes out of an oral program, he ought to have more speech.

When this father said he wanted his son to do "the best possible" he wasn't referring to academic achievement or social and emotional development. He wanted his son to be normal and to integrate into the hearing world.

The combined teacher maintains that good speech will only come as the result of a strong language base. Language, in the combined teacher's view, is the substance, and signs and speech are merely the vehicles of its expression.

The importance of early communication and language development is not questioned by most educators, be they combinists or oralists. The latter may admit that oralism sacrifices a degree of early communication, but they are willing to risk this loss in order to gain better oral skills in the long run. One oralist expressed it as follows:

It's one of the risks you take when you choose oralism. We don't know when and to what extent this deprivation to the child of the means to communicate—how it is going to show up when he grows up. We'll just have to wait and see.

What is "Normal?"

One might think that the importance of early language development would prove to be a compelling case for sign language. However, oralists still claim, as did Bell, that the use of signs "marks" a person as being different and frustrates the effort to "normalize" the individual. One mother spoke at length about a child she knew who had been through a combined program and was able to get work only as a mail sorter. As a result, the child was very "unhappy." When the mother was asked if she thought sign language was responsible for the child's unhappiness, she responded, "of course. I think sign language is very beautiful; I like to watch it. But for living in this world, give me as much oralism as possible."

Bell and Gallaudet disagreed over what constituted normal behavior and normal society and how deaf people fit into that society. Bell believed normal meant being as much like hearing people as possible. Deaf people could become active, fulfilled members of society if they could communicate like hearing people. Gallaudet equated normal with educational attainment and moral development. With the proper intellectual and moral training, deaf people could find themselves happy and productive members of society. These differing views of normality still exist within the field of education of deaf children. The underlying foundation of oral education still seems to be the striving to be a part of "normal society." This goal is particularly appealing to teachers and parents alike. As an oral teacher put it,

> What I got from oral training was, "Yes, you're deaf, that's too bad isn't it? But you've got to function in this world. If you want to wallow in deafness and how awful it is, okay, but we're not going to put up with that." I've seen a lot of hearing-impaired kids who develop beautiful oral skills. I hate to think of kids being deprived of that skill. To give them the chance to be some percentage normal, to fit into the regular world, that's what I'd like to do.

Combinists argue that oralists, in their effort to make children normal, actually subject them to abnormal situations. Is the ability to speak, they ask, more important than the establishment of a positive self-image? A teacher said,

> I think of the kids who are mainstreamed [integrated] and what their options are for having close friendships and meaningful relationships. I look at kids going into programs maybe being able to follow the teacher, having maybe one or two friends that they can communicate with, but still being real isolated.

Oralists respond that oral education does not mean a loss of meaningful relationships, nor does it mean a denial of deafness. In truth, however, communication through sign language with other deaf people is so important to the deaf individual that the prohibition of signing must be considered a denial or devaluation of the deaf subculture. Note this exchange with a teacher at an oral school:

Question: Does the oral method deny the individual his or her
            identity as a deaf person?

Answer: No. I lived in the dormitory for five years. I talked
            with those kids, I knew them, I lived with them day in
            and day out. If there's one thing they knew, they knew
            they were deaf. The kids would get together at 11 or 12
            at night, they'd all go into somebody's room and they'd
            sit and gesture and sign.

Question: Then there was signing at the school?

Answer: Not officially, but there was signing in the dorms. At a
            time like that they'd get together, and that was their
            way of saying, "See, we're deaf."

This is a good example of how oralism inhibits the formation of a
deaf identity, even though it was offered by the teacher to prove just
the opposite. That children must meet covertly in dormitory rooms in
the middle of the night, just so they can communicate in sign language,
indicates a poor environment for the formation of a positive self-image.

The debate over what is normal must, of necessity, include the
viewpoint of the deaf subculture or deaf community. This community
is comprised of social and athletic clubs, state associations, summer camps,
cultural activities, and other events and groups organized by and for
deaf people. The deaf participants find a special sense of belonging in
this community; they intermarry and identify themselves as a group.

Bell feared the existence of such a group identity. To him it represented a failure to integrate, and it practically ensured the existence
of more deaf people through intermarriage. Many oralists still view the
deaf community as the home of "deaf failures" (i.e., those who were not
successful in oral programs). One proponent of that view offered the
following explanation for the growth of the deaf community:

We're in the "Me" generation right now. We'll be leaving that eventually because the world doesn't function as me-first always. As appealing as the deaf culture is to many deaf people right now, I'm afraid
that they will learn that they still have to function in the hearing world.
One of the reasons that the deaf have come into their own right now,
with the deaf power thing, is that society in general is much more a
"Me" society—"What's good for me? I don't really give a damn about
my neighbors. I'm thinking about me."

The underlying premise of this argument is widely held among oral educators: "Normal society is better than the deaf community, and deaf students should be prepared to find a place in it. Society would be a better place if the deaf community did not exist and the deaf took their place alongside their hearing peers." When this thought was put to an advocate of the combined method, his response included an analysis of the oralists' definition of normality.

> I think that those people and I would have disagreements about a lot of communities that exist, about differences and similarities, and about wanting to mainstream people to be ... normal, middle class, talking, hearing, white. Difference is good. I think the basic disagreement people have on this kind of controversy is: What is difference all about, and can you accept people who are different from you? And can they exist, not exactly like you do, but still be okay? I think oralists have difficulty accepting a lot of those communities.

Oral educators might respond that individual differences should be respected, but not to the detriment of the larger society. Bell made the same argument, and in many ways it is compelling. The quest for normality should not be considered in a purely negative light. It is, unfortunately, human nature to look askance at those whom we perceive as being different or deviant. When a personal relationship is lacking, judgments about people are often made on the basis of less significant factors, such as dress, manners, and other outward manifestations of what some see as inner attributes (e.g., intelligence, ethnic background, social status). All schools are nothing else if not centers of socialization and normalization. One may argue whether schools should play this role, but few deny that it is a major outcome of public schooling in the United States. Given this state of affairs, it is not unreasonable to expect that schools for deaf children should also play a normalizing role.

A problem arises when striving for normalization occurs at the expense of the integrity and positive self-image of the individual. Consider the case of residential schools: Because some deaf children spend the majority of their time at these schools, it seems reasonable that the schools teach grooming and social skills. Proper social behavior may demand the prohibition of gestures that are considered antisocial (or abnormal). But who determines the correctness or normality of individual gestures? Deaf people communicate with gestures even in oral environments, though such communication may be covert. If the value of socialization conflicts with the value of individual expression, which should take priority? This and other questions are the same ones that generated debate in the 1800s: Does sign language prevent integration and thus promote a deaf subculture? Does the existence of that subculture harm deaf people? Is the deaf subculture bad for society by perpetuating a deviant population? Would, in short, the world be a better place if no deaf people were in it?

These questions are at the root of the sign language debate. They have not been fully addressed, and so the debate continues, as does the antagonism that accompanies it. An oralist, speaking of teachers who use the combined method, described them as being

> more interested in their time off, and what's going to be easy to teach to a child, what's going to get across faster; what will give them, as teachers, more immediate gratification.... What they're doing, as I see it, is imposing their interests and their feelings on the kids.

A combinist, describing oralists, said, "It just seems that those people overlook reality. They say, "We're going to make them into hearing kids, we're going to make them talk." They try and try and try, and [the kids] don't talk anyway. They're ignoring reality."

These emotional generalizations about "the other side" are all too common among professionals who teach deaf children. Everyone feels that their way is the correct way, and parents and children get caught in the middle.

The Need for Change

During the last two hundred years the intensity of the communications debate has wavered but has never died. Nor will it, as long as teachers, parents, and policymakers disagree about the purpose of educating deaf children. Those who see it as a means for children to achieve their full potential as individuals through intellectual and social development will probably insist on sign language. Those who view it as a form of socialization and an opportunity for students to fit into normal society will probably go the oral route. Total harmony thus appears unlikely.

If an end to the debate is ever to come, it will probably be a result of modern technology. For example, cochlear implants now make it possible for a small number of hearing-impaired people to have their hearing improved. It is possible that further developments with this technology will eventually reduce the number of students in schools and classes for hearing-impaired children. More sophisticated postnatal tests may allow for earlier identification and aural remediation of hearing loss, again decreasing the need for special instruction. There is even the chance that prenatal testing, through earlier and improved amniocentesis, will someday identify genetic deafness months before birth.

This last technology, amniocentesis, puts the entire problem squarely on the line. Once a fetus has been determined to have a profound hearing loss, parents would be faced with a choice—they could continue the pregnancy with the knowledge that their child would be deaf, or they could choose to have an abortion. This hypothetical situation is already being experienced by prospective parents of children with Down's syndrome and some other genetic abnormalities. The question arises of what one should do in the case of a potentially deaf child. In this matter the question is not over communications, but over life itself. For now the question is one of philosophy—tomorrow it may be painfully real.

Despite recent advances in technology, the education of deaf children today remains remarkably the same as it was in Bell's and Gallaudet's time. Though electronic advancements have created powerful hearing aids and sophisticated testing equipment, the actual teaching of deaf children has changed little. New systems for teaching language and speech have come and gone, new sign language systems have been developed, and a variety of administrative and organizational schemes have been employed at residential schools and within public school systems. The fact remains that large numbers of deaf children are still taught in state-supported residential schools whose physical characteristics, like their teaching methods, resemble those of the late 1800s. Many other children are being taught as Bell had envisioned (i.e., within normal public schools). The reality, however, is often less a move toward the mainstream than it is a cost-effective charade. These mainstreamed classes frequently include minimal interaction with regular students; actual integration occurs only during lunch periods and outside exercise. The mere physical presence of hearing-impaired children in a school does not guarantee normalization. In fact, this experience can actually be negative for youngsters if efforts to sensitize and educate teachers, students, and parents from the hearing population are not made.

Now, more than ever, a dialogue is needed. In the past, the invisibleness of deafness—due to the lack of outward signs of a handicap—caused some educators and legislators to overlook its serious consequences. This led to inadequate programs and underserved or unserved children. Today, government policies for handicapped people are increasingly being determined by the economy and not by the needs of children. The emphasis on cost-effective planning will undoubtedly continue throughout the 1980s, with serious implications for the education of deaf children. In their efforts to save money, policymakers may repeat their past mistakes. Forced migrations of deaf students from special programs or classes into regular classrooms would save money and demonstrate commitment to the normalization of deaf students. The temptation to implement such a campaign, without taking the needs and abilities of the individual children into consideration, presents a challenge to educators.

Advocates must speak out on behalf of deaf children and their families in order that the true needs of the students be recognized and met. They must speak as one voice, not through splintered factions that seek to protect their own turf. It is inevitable, and perhaps desirable, that financially strapped educators will put an end to dual systems that offer separate oral and combined programs. When this happens, will oral and combined advocates focus their efforts against each other, or will they work together to meet the needs of children in a unified way?

No single method of communication as presently practiced can meet all of the needs of all deaf students. This is as true now as it was in the days of Bell and Gallaudet. The only way to moderate the communication schism is to recognize its roots and to understand that attitudes toward deviancy and expectations for deaf individuals are important factors. In time, arguments may shift away from "which system is best for all" to "which system is best for each individual child." This won't resolve the debate, but it will at least provide a starting point for future discussion. If, as has been written, history is an argument without end, we can at least move beyond the beginning.

Notes

CHAPTER ONE

1. Alexander Graham Bell, "The Growth of the Oral Method in America" (Speech given at the 15th anniversary ceremony of the Clarke School for the Deaf, Northampton, Massachusetts, October 10, 1917), 20–21, Bell Collection, Library of Congress.
2. Harvey Peet, "Memoir on the Origin and Early History of the Art of Instructing the Deaf and Dumb," *American Annals of the Deaf* 3 (1851): 141.
3. K. Hodgson, *The Deaf and Their Problems* (New York: Philosophical Library, 1954).
4. Ruth Bender, *The Conquest of Deafness* (Cleveland: Case Western Reserve University, 1970).
5. Juan P. Bonet, *Reducion de las letras y arte para ensenar a hablar los mudos* (Madrid: Par Francisco Arbaco de Angelo, 1620).
6. Beryl L. Benderly, *Dancing Without Music: Deafness in America* (Garden City, NY: Anchor Press/Doubleday, 1980), 110.
7. C. Garnet, ed., *The Exchange of Letters Between Samuel Heinicke and Abbe Charles Michel de l'Epee* (New York: Vantage Press, 1968).
8. Robert Bruce, *Alexander Graham Bell and the Conquest of Solitude* (Boston: Little, Brown, 1973), 85.
9. American Asylum, at Hartford, for the Education and Instruction of the Deaf and Dumb, *Twenty Ninth Report* (Hartford, CT: American Asylum, 1845): 78.
10. Ibid., 88.
11. Donald Moores, *Educating the Deaf: Psychology, Principles, and Practices* (Boston: Houghton Mifflin, 1978), 33.

CHAPTER TWO

1. J. Hitz, "Alexander Melville Bell," *The Association Review* 7 (1905): 423–424.
2. "New Tool for Training the Deaf," *London Illustrated Times* (September 1864).
3. Alexander Graham Bell to his parents, May 23, 1871, Bell Family Papers, Library of Congress.
4. Robert Bruce, *Alexander Graham Bell and the Conquest of Solitude* (Boston: Little, Brown, 1973), 81.
5. Bruce, *Bell*, 88.
6. Mabel Hubbard Bell, Diary, January 6, 1879, Bell Family Papers.
7. A. G. Bell to M. H. Bell, November 22, 1876, Bell Family Papers.

8. L. Ward, "Handicapped Children in Our Public Schools, *Wisconsin Journal of Education* (March 1936): 329.
9. Helen Keller, *The Story of My Life* (Garden City, NY: Doubleday, 1954), 18–19.
10. A. G. Bell, "The Education of the Deaf," (unpublished manuscript, October 28, 1889), 1, Bell Family Papers.
11. Ibid.
12. A. G. Bell, "Fallacies Concerning the Deaf," *American Annals of the Deaf* 29, (1884): 44.
13. A. G. Bell, "Utility of Signs," *Educator* (May 1894): 11.
14. Bell, "Fallacies," 47–48.
15. Ibid., 52.
16. Ibid., 39.
17. Ibid., 46.
18. Bell, "Utility," 21.

CHAPTER THREE

1. Edward Miner Gallaudet, Presidential Address, 1864, Gallaudet Family Papers, Library of Congress.
2. Gallaudet, Memoirs, n.d., Gallaudet Papers.
3. Gallaudet, Diary, July 12, 1857, Gallaudet Papers.
4. Ibid., December 1865.
5. J. Sullivan to M. T. Boatner, [undated], Gallaudet Papers.
6. Gallaudet, "Report of the President on the Systems of Deaf-Mute Instruction Pursued in Europe," *Annual Report of the Columbia Institution* (1867): 54 (Gallaudet University Archives, Washington, DC).
7. Gallaudet, Journal, April 1865, Gallaudet Papers.
8. Gallaudet, "The American System of Deaf-Mute Instruction—Its Incidental Defects and Their Remedies," *American Annals of the Deaf* 13 (1868): 150.
9. Ibid., 170.
10. Ibid., 154–155.
11. Gallaudet, "Is the Sign Language Used to Excess in Teaching Deaf-Mutes?," *American Annals of the Deaf* 16 (1871): 27.
12. Gallaudet, "Must the Sign Language Go?," *American Annals of the Deaf* 44 (1899): 228.
13. Ibid.
14. Gallaudet, "The Value of Sign Language to the Deaf," *American Annals of the Deaf* 32 (1877): 145.
15. "The Problems of Orally-Taught Deaf," New York *Evening Post*, April 24, 1895.
16. Gallaudet, "The Proper Adjustment of Methods in the Education of the Deaf" (Paper presented at the World's Congress of Instructors of the Deaf, Chicago, July 1893); Gallaudet University Archives, Washington, DC.

CHAPTER FOUR

1. Alexander Graham Bell to Edward Miner Gallaudet, 1887, Bell Papers Library of Congress.
2. Bell to Gallaudet, November 29, 1889, Bell Papers.
3. Gallaudet to Bell, December 3, 1889, Bell Papers.
4. J. Gordon, ed., *Evidence of Edward Miner Gallaudet and Alexander Graham Bell Presented to the Royal Commission of the United Kingdom* (Washington, DC: Volta Bureau, 1892), 42–43.
5. Gallaudet, Diary, January 24, 1891, Gallaudet Papers, Library of Congress.
6. Ibid., January 25, 1891.
7. Ibid., January 26, 1891.
8. Bell, "Teaching the Deaf and Dumb" (Statement before the House Appropriations Committee, 1891; Bell Papers), 1–2.
9. Ibid., 7–8.
10. Ibid., 7.
11. Gallaudet, Diary, January 27, 1891, Gallaudet Papers.
12. J. R. Dobyns to Bell, February 17, 1891, Bell Papers.
13. Bell to Dobyns, February 21, 1891, Bell Papers.
14. Gallaudet, Diary, February 16, 1891, Gallaudet Papers.
15. Ibid., February 19, 1891.
16. Ibid., February 21, 1891.
17. Ibid., February 23, 1891.
18. Ibid., February 24, 1891.
19. Ibid., March 4, 1891.
20. Robert Bruce, *Alexander Graham Bell and the Conquest of Solitude* (Boston: Little, Brown, 1973), 387.
21. Gallaudet, Diary, March 8, 1891, Gallaudet Papers.

CHAPTER FIVE

1. Edward Miner Gallaudet, "College Correspondence," *The Companion* (March 1891; Bell Papers, Library of Congress).
2. Alexander Graham Bell to Gallaudet, March 16, 1891, Bell Papers.
3. A. G. Bell to Mabel Hubbard Bell, March 16, 1891, Bell Papers.
4. M. H. Bell to A. G. Bell, March 17, 1891, Bell Papers.
5. A. G. Bell to M. H. Bell, March 18, 1891, Bell Papers.
6. Gallaudet to A. G. Bell, March 18, 1891, Bell Papers.
7. A. G. Bell to M. H. Bell, March 19, 1891, Bell Papers.
8. Ibid.
9. Gallaudet, Diary, March 19, 1891, Gallaudet Papers, Library of Congress.
10. Ibid., March 21, 1891.
11. Gallaudet to A. G. Bell, March 23, 1891, Bell Papers.
12. A. G. Bell to Gallaudet, March 30, 1891, Bell Papers.
13. Ibid.

14. Ibid.
15. Gallaudet to A. G. Bell, March 31, 1891, Bell Papers.
16. A. G. Bell to Gallaudet, April 1, 1891, Bell Papers.
17. A. W. McCurdy to Gallaudet, April 3, 1891, Bell Papers.
18. A. G. Bell to Gallaudet, April 3, 1891 (a), Bell Papers.
19. A. G. Bell to Gallaudet, April 3, 1891 (b), Bell Papers.
20. Gallaudet to A. G. Bell, April 3, 1891, Bell Papers.
21. A. G. Bell to Gallaudet, April 4, 1891, Bell Papers.
22. Gallaudet, Diary, April 11, 1891, Gallaudet Papers.
23. A. G. Bell to A. E. Crouter, April 1, 1892, Bell Papers.
24. Maxine T. Boatner, *Voice of the Deaf* (Washington, DC: Public Affairs Press, 1959), 137.
25. Ibid., 138.
26. G. McClure, "Dr. Edward Miner Gallaudet as I Remember Him," *Just Once a Month* 29(4) (1950): 3; 12–13.
27. Robert Bruce, *Alexander Graham Bell and the Conquest of Solitude* (Boston: Little, Brown, 1973), 338.
28. Sarah Fuller to M. H. Bell, August 31, 1895, Bell Papers.
29. G. McClure to W. McClure, February 6, 1950, Gallaudet Papers.
30. A. G. Bell to M. H. Bell, July 22, 1895, Bell Papers.
31. M. H. Bell to A. G. Bell, March 12, 1896, Bell Papers.
32. A. G. Bell to M. H. Bell, March 17, 1896, Bell Papers.
33. Bruce, *Bell*, 389.
34. Donald Moores, *Educating the Deaf: Psychology, Principles, and Practices* (Boston: Houghton Mifflin, 1978) 64.

CHAPTER SIX

1. J. Hitz, "Alexander Melville Bell," *Association Review* 7 (1905): 423.
2. Alexander Graham Bell, "Beinn Bhreagh Recorder" (Unpublished paper, November 5, 1909; Bell Papers, Library of Congress), 73–78.
3. Ibid.
4. Bell, "Notes of Early Life," *Volta Review* 12 (1910): 156–157.
5. Edward Miner Gallaudet, Diary, April 20, 1856, Gallaudet Papers, Library of Congress.
6. Mrs. G. Grosvenor, "Mrs. Alexander Graham Bell—A Reminiscence," *Volta Review* 59 (1957): 299–305.
7. Bell, "Beinn Bhreagh Recorder" (Unpublished paper, February 24, 1919; Bell Papers), 1–21.
8. Carolyn Yale, "Mabel Hubbard Bell, 1859–1923," *Volta Review* 25 (1923): 107–110.
9. Mabel Hubbard Bell, "World of Silence" (Unpublished paper, n.d.; Bell Papers).
10. Amos Draper, "Sophia Gallaudet," *American Annals of the Deaf* 22 (1877): 172.

11. Ibid., 174.
12. Ibid., 175.
13. Ibid., 178.
14. Gallaudet, Diary, December 31, 1866, Gallaudet Papers.
15. Ibid., January 12, 1872.

CHAPTER SEVEN

1. For a more complete explanation of Social Darwinism, see Daniel Kevles, *In the Name of Eugenics: Genetics and the Uses of Human Heredity* (New York: Alfred Knopf, 1985); Mark Haller, *Eugenics: Hereditarian Attitudes in American Thought* (New Brunswick, NJ: Rutgers Univeristy Press, 1963); and Richard Hofstadter, *Social Darwinism in American Thought*, rev. ed. (Boston Press, 1955).
2. Alexander Graham Bell, "How to Improve the Race," *Journal of Heredity* 5 (1914): 4–6.
3. Ibid.: 6–7.
4. A. G. Bell to D. Fairchild, November 23, 1908, Bell Papers, Library of Congress.
5. A. G. Bell, "A Few Thoughts Concerning Eugenics," *National Geographic* (February 1908): 121–122.
6. Ibid.: 119.
7. Mabel Hubbard Bell, Diary, January 6, 1879, Bell Papers.
8. A. G. Bell, "A Few Thoughts," 123.
9. Ibid.
10. A. G. Bell, "Is Race Suicide Possible?" *Journal of Heredity* 11, (1920): 340.
11. Ibid., 341.
12. A. G. Bell, "Beinn Bhreagh Recorder" (Unpublished paper, April 19, 1915; Bell Papers), 345–346.
13. Ibid. (December 1, 1911), 432–436.
14. Ibid.
15. A. G. Bell, "How to Improve the Race," 1–2.
16. A. G. Bell, "Thoughts Concerning Eugenics," 120.
17. A. G. Bell, "Beinn Bhreagh Recorder" (Unpublished paper, August 31, 1914; Bell Papers), 234.
18. Ibid., 225; 228.
19. A. G. Bell to Fairchild, November 23, 1908, Bell Papers.
20. Ibid.
21. Ibid.
22. A. G. Bell, "Beinn Bhreagh Recorder" (Unpublished paper, December 26, 1914; Bell Papers), 160–165.
23. A. G. Bell, "Beinn Bhreagh Recorder" (Unpublished paper, December 26, 1914; Bell Papers), 152–159.
24. A. G. Bell, "Thoughts Concerning Eugenics," 122–123.

25. Robert Bruce, *Alexander Graham Bell and the Conquest of Solitude* (Boston: Little, Brown, 1973), 308.

26. Ibid.

27. M. H. Bell to A. G. Bell, July 9, 1895, Bell Papers.

28. A. G. Bell, *Memoir Upon the Formation of a Deaf Variety of the Human Race* (Washington, DC: Government Printing Office, 1884; Washington, DC: A. G. Bell Association for the Deaf, 1969).

29. Ibid., 48.

30. Ibid., 46.

31. Ibid.

32. A. G. Bell to Edward Fay, October 27, 1890, Bell Papers.

33. A. G. Bell, "Professor A. Graham Bell's Studies of the Deaf," *Science* (September 1890): 135–136.

34. A. G. Bell to M. H. Bell, May 5, 1890, Bell Papers.

35. A. G. Bell, "Marriage: An Address to the Deaf" (Unpublished speech, March 6, 1891; Bell Papers).

36. Ibid.

37. Ibid.

38. Ibid.

39. A. G. Bell to J. R. Dobyns, February 21, 1891, Bell Papers.

40. A. G. Bell, "Growth of the Oral Method of Instructing the Deaf," *Annual Report of the Committee on the Horace Mann School* (1895; Bell Papers).

41. I. King Jordan, Gerilee Gustason, and Roslyn Rosen, "An Update on Communication Trends at Programs for the Deaf," *American Annals of the Deaf* 124 (1979): 350–357.

42. Edward Miner Gallaudet, "Deaf-Mutism," *American Annals of the Deaf* 20 (1875): 231–232.

43. Gallaudet, "The Aim of the Education of the Deaf," *American Annals of the Deaf* 38 (1893): 206.

44. Gallaudet, "Values in the Education of the Deaf" (Paper presented at the Seventh Biannual Meeting of the Conference of Superintendents and Principals of American Schools for the Deaf, Colorado Springs, August 1892).

45. A. G. Bell, "Fallacies Concerning the Deaf," *American Annals of the Deaf* 29 (1884): 69.

46. Gallaudet, "The Education of the Deaf: Its Opportunities and Perils" (Paper presented at the World's Congress of Instructors of the Deaf, Chicago, July 1893; Gallaudet University Archives, Washington, DC).

47. Gallaudet, "Deaf-Mute Conventions, Associations, and Newspapers," *American Annals of the Deaf* 18 (1873): 200.

48. Gallaudet, "Values in Education," 19.

49. Gallaudet, "The Ideal School for the Deaf," *American Annals of the Deaf* 37 (1892): 284.

50. A. G. Bell to M. H. Bell, January 17, 1876, Bell Papers.

51. Gallaudet, "Values in Education," 15.

52. Gallaudet, "What Is Speech Worth to the Deaf?" (Privately printed paper, 1900; Gallaudet University Archives, Washington, DC), 10.
53. Ibid., 11.
54. Ibid.
55. Gallaudet, Diary, February 5, 1891, Gallaudet Papers, Library of Congress.
56. Ibid., March 8, 1891.
57. Gallaudet, "Education of the Deaf," 15.
58. Gallaudet, "Marriage," *American Annals of the Deaf* 36 (1891): 82.
59. Ibid., 83.

Selected Bibliography

WORKS BY ALEXANDER GRAHAM BELL

Bell Family Papers	Manuscript Division, Library of Congress, Washington, DC.
Bell, A. G. 1872	Visible speech as a means of communicating articulation to deaf-mutes. *American Annals of the Deaf*, 17, 1–21.
1884	Fallacies concerning the deaf. *American Annals of the Deaf*, 29, 32–69.
1884	*Upon the formation of a deaf variety of the human race.* Washington, DC: Government Printing Office.
1890, September	Professor A. Graham Bell's studies of the deaf. *Science*, pp. 135–136.
1894	Utility of signs. *Educator*, 5, 3–23.
1896	*Growth of the oral method of instructing the deaf.* Boston: Press of Rockwell & Churchill.
1898	*Marriage: An address to the deaf.* Washington, DC: Sanders Printing Office.
1908	A few thoughts concerning eugenics. *National Geographic*, 19, 119–123.
1914	How to improve the race. *Journal of Heredity*, 5, 1–7.
1917	*Graphical studies of marriages of the deaf.* Washington, DC: Volta Bureau.
1918	*The duration of life and conditions associated with longevity.* Washington, DC: Genealogical Record Office.
1919	Who shall inherit long life? *National Geographic*, 35, 505–514.
1920	Is race suicide possible? *Journal of Heredity*, 11, 339–341.

WORKS ABOUT THE BELL FAMILY

Bruce, R.
1973
Alexander Graham Bell and the conquest of solitude. Boston: Little, Brown.

Burlingame, R.
1964
Out of silence into sound: The life of Alexander Graham Bell. New York: Macmillan.

Costain, T.
1960
The chord of steel. Garden City, NY: Doubleday.

Curry, S.
1909
Alexander Melville Bell: Some memories, with fragments from a pupil's notebook. Boston: School of Expression.

Grosvenor, E.
1951
My father, Alexander Graham Bell. *Volta Review,* 53, 349, 386–388.

Grosvenor, G.
1957
Mrs. Alexander Graham Bell—A reminiscence. *Volta Review,* 59, 299–305.

Grosvenor, M.
1940
Memories of my grandfather. *Volta Review,* 42, 621–622.

Mackenzie, C.
1928
Alexander Graham Bell, the man who contracted space. Boston: Houghton Mifflin.

Mitchell, S.
1971
The haunting influence of Alexander Graham Bell. *American Annals of the Deaf,* 116, 349–356.

Waite, H.
1961
Make a joyful sound. Philadelphia: Macrae Smith.

Yale, C.
1923
Mabel Hubbard Bell—1859–1923. *Volta Review,* 25, 107–110.

WORKS BY EDWARD MINER GALLAUDET

Gallaudet
Collection
Gallaudet University Archives, Washington, DC.

Gallaudet
Family Papers
Manuscript Division, Library of Congress, Washington, DC.

Gallaudet, E. M. 1868	The American system of deaf-mute instruction—Its incidental defects and their remedies. *American Annals of the Deaf*, 13, 147–170.
1871	Is sign language used to excess in teaching deaf-mutes? *American Annals of the Deaf*, 16, 26–33.
1875	Deaf-mutism. *American Annals of the Deaf* 20, 230–248.
1887	The value of sign language to the deaf. *American Annals of the Deaf*, 32, 141–147.
1888	*Life of Thomas Hopkins Gallaudet*. New York: Henry Holt.
1892	The ideal school for the deaf. *American Annals of the Deaf*, 37, 280–285.
1899	Must the sign language go? *American Annals of the Deaf*, 44, 221–229.
1912	A history of the Columbian Institution for the Deaf and Dumb. *Columbia Historical Society Records*, 15, 1–22.

WORKS ABOUT THE GALLAUDET FAMILY

Barnard, H. 1852	*Tribute to Gallaudet*. Hartford: Brockett & Hutchinson.
Boatner, M. 1959	*Voice of the deaf*. Washington, DC: Public Affairs Press.
Draper, A. 1877	Sophia Gallaudet. *American Annals of the Deaf*, 22, 170–183.
Humphrey, H. 1877	*The life and labors of the Rev. Thomas H. Gallaudet*. New York: R. Carten & Brothers.

WORKS ON DEAFNESS

| Benderly, B. 1980 | *Dancing without music: Deafness in America*. Garden City, NY: Anchor Press/Doubleday. |
| Best, H. 1914 | *The deaf*. New York: T. Y. Crowell. |

1943   *Deafness and the deaf in the United States.* New York: MacMillan.

Bulwer, J.   *Philocophus; Or, the deafe and dumbe man's friend.* London:
1648   Humphrey Moseley.

Calkins, E.   *Louder please: The autobiography of a deaf man.* Boston: At-
1924   lantic Monthly Press.

DeLand, F.   *The story of lipreading* (rev. ed.). Washington, DC: Volta Bu-
1968   reau.

Garnet, C.   *The exchange of letters between Samuel Heinicke and Abbé*
1968   *Charles Michael de l'Epée.* New York: Vantage.

Lane, H.   *When the mind hears: A history of the deaf.* New York: Random
1984   House.

Yale, C.   *Years of building.* New York: Dial Press.
1931

WORKS ON DEVIANCY AND NORMALITY

Barr, M.   *Mental defectives: Their history, treatment and training.* New
1973   York: Arno Press.

Bronfenbrenner,   The origins of alienation. *Scientific American*, 53–61.
U.
1974, August

Garnette, C.   *The world of silence: A new venture in philosophy.* New York:
1967   Greenwich.

Goffman, I.   *Stigma: Notes on the management of spoiled identity.* Englewood
1963   Cliffs, NJ: Prentice-Hall.

Hobbs, N.   *The futures of children.* San Francisco: Jossey-Bass.
1974

Kevles, D.   *In the name of eugenics: Genetics and the uses of human heredity.*
1985   New York: Knopf.

Kirp, D.   Student classification, public policy and the courts. *Harvard*
1974   *Educational Review*, 44, 7–52.

Kittrie, N.
1971
The right to be different. Baltimore: Johns Hopkins University Press.

Lane, H.
1976
The wild boy of Aveyron. Cambridge: Harvard University Press.

Lane, H., &
Pillard, R.
1978
The wild boy of Burundi. New York: Random House.

Malson, L.
1972
Wolf children and the problem of human nature. New York: Monthly Review Press.

Rainwater, L.
(Ed.)
1974
Deviance and liberty. Chicago: Aldine.

Rothman, D.
1971
The discovery of the asylum: Social order and disorder in the new republic. Boston: Little, Brown.

Whitney, L.
1934
The case for sterilization. New York: Frederick Stokes.

Wolfensberger,
W.
1972
Normalization: The principle of normalization in human services. Toronto: National Institute on Mental Retardation.

Index

This book was set in 11/13 Granjon by
Techna-Type, Inc. of York, PA. It was
printed on 60 lb Glatfelter Offset,
an acid-free paper. The jacket and text
were designed by Wayne Caravella.